AN INTRODUCTION TO

P & I

by

CHRISTOPHER HILL
MA (Oxon), FICS

BILL ROBERTSON
FICS, ACIArb

STEVEN J. HAZELWOOD
LLB, LLM, PhD, ACIArb

LLP

LONDON NEW YORK HAMBURG HONG KONG
LLOYD'S OF LONDON PRESS LTD
1988

Lloyd's of London Press Ltd
Legal Publishing and Conferences Division
One Singer Street, London EC2A 4LQ

USA AND CANADA
Lloyd's of London Press Inc
Suite 523, 611 Broadway
New York, NY 10012, USA

GERMANY
Lloyd's of London Press GmbH
59 Ehrenbergstrasse, 2000 Hamburg 50
West Germany

SOUTH EAST ASIA
Lloyd's of London Press (Far East) Ltd
903 Chung Nam Building
1 Lockhart Road, Wanchai
Hong Kong

First published in Great Britain 1988

British Library Cataloguing in Publication Data
Hill, Christopher
An introduction to P & I
1. Shipping. Insurance in Great Britain
I. Title II. Robertson, Bill III. Hazelwood, Steven J.
368.2'2'00941

ISBN 1–85044–163–4

Text set in 11pt on 12pt Plantin by
Wessex Typesetters, Frome, Somerset
Printed in Great Britain by
Bookcraft Ltd, Midsomer Norton

PREFACE

We three co-authors would like to leave no doubts in the minds of those who may read this book as to what are its purpose, scope and, above all, limitations. In other words, we believe it to be important to warn prospective readers about what it is not, rather than to outline to them what it is. Most importantly, this is not a comprehensive 'guided tour' of the mysteries of each of the individual P & I associations. The three of us have been very careful to avoid any drawing of comparisons between one club and another, the making of any distinction between the rules of one club and those of another. Secondly, it is not a law book and few law cases are quoted. It is a practical book, an analysis in reasonable depth of a particular and very specialised type of insurance, third-party liability insurance of shipowners and others and also allied insurances within the framework of the marine industry.

Two out of the three of us have spent a large slice of our working lives on the payroll of one or other of what are described in this book as the 'group clubs'. Our loyalties were, during those periods, necessarily bound to our clubs and had we still been working for those clubs, this book would, in all probability, never have become a reality. It is remarkable that there has never been a book on P & I insurance generally. There have been odd chapters here and there in sundry books on marine insurance, there have been guidebooks and handbooks compiled and issued by club managers which combined an explanatory purpose with an advertising role and thus do not equate with the more generalised and objective approach of this book.

Much of the material from which this book derives its existence was originally produced by Steven Hazelwood. He, of the three of us, had been the academic before rejoining the fold in the City. During his academic period he conducted research into the workings of P & I clubs and on completion the research was written up into three stiff-backed weighty volumes; something of an encyclopaedia. What it did not contain about P & I clubs was not worth including; it could be described as the next best thing to perfection. We, the two 'club men', Bill Robertson and I, initially had a mind to condense it, but this would not of itself have produced what we wanted which was more of a practical introductory guide to the clubs. The following is the result of our efforts based on Steven Hazelwood's original text.

Few people outside the P & I world have much idea what P & I means, let alone what P & I insurance covers, for whom, and why. It is our hope and certainly our aim that those uninitiated in the mysteries of P & I will find the answers to whatever their questions may be in the pages which follow. We assure our readers that they will not be swamped in academia, nor slither on ice floes of legal niceties nor choke on an endless intake of law cases.

We should like to take this opportunity to thank Mrs Irene Edwards, Mrs Anita Collins and Mrs Dawn Morgan for the good humoured way in which they have so patiently processed all the various alterations and additions to this book. Without their cheerful assistance our rate of production would have plummeted to low levels.

September 1988

CHRISTOPHER HILL
BILL ROBERTSON
STEVEN HAZELWOOD

CONTENTS

I

ORIGINS AND HISTORY OF THE CLUBS

The original concept of combination as an early experiment in risk sharing most probably arose out of the natural herding instinct of men finding the advantages to be gained in companionship with their fellows.

Numerous accounts exist in history of ancient mutual devices and an example of early risk sharing is of Chinese river merchants 'averaging' their losses by means of distributing their cargoes over a number of vessels and loading half of their cargoes on each other's vessels, thereby dividing or spreading the risk of loss. There were also the guilds or Ras of India, Babylonia, Chaldea, Egypt and Phoenicia. From these very crude beginnings there developed a more sophisticated system whereby societies, guilds, clubs and associations were developed by the Greeks and Romans. Societies can also be traced which were more clearly mutual insurance associations providing for life insurance, burial expenses, and indeed protection from various other dangers.

Parallels can be drawn from the running of these ancient clubs when compared with the practices of the modern-day P & I associations. For example, management was in the hands of a committee elected by and drawn from the membership and the club was financed by way of periodic subscriptions and contributions made when needed to meet unexpected expenses. There is even evidence of reinsurance between Roman burial clubs by means of a pooling arrangement and rules providing for the settlement of disputes by arbitration. Withdrawal of cover in cases of misconduct were also prevalent in respect of which further parallels can be drawn with the terms and provisions found in the rules of modern P & I associations.

THE MIDDLE AGES

In the Mediterranean and Adriatic regions many examples exist of partnerships of risks and further north there is evidence of Danish and German guilds for shipowners, the best known of these being the guilds of Flanders. It may also be said that the famous Hanseatic league, a combination for mutual protection, was in itself a form of mutual insurance association.

Most of the German guilds were concerned with the most dominant peril of fire on land, but there are traces of marine insurance conducted on mutual lines in Italy and Venice in particular and also in Portugal and The Netherlands.

THE BRITISH SCENE

Important developments in the concept of mutual insurance were made in the Mediaeval period which centred on the guilds. Whether these guilds were of Anglo-Saxon origin or whether the Saxons found them here and shaped them to conform with their own institutions is not clear but by the Middle Ages there were guilds providing, either as a dominant aspect, or as a subsidiary function, insurance in respect of theft of cattle, fire, poverty and death. These institutions reached their peak of popularity in this country in the 13th and 14th centuries in the form of craft guilds offering as a sideline benefits in cases of sickness and death and by combination to mitigate the general misfortunes of life. By the 18th century there was a transformation from the guild to the 'friendly society' providing support in the case of death, injury and other perils and misfortunes of every day life. A concept of brotherhood and neighbourly help was also applied to the dangers of sailing a ship and the hull clubs of the 18th and 19th centuries were born of this spirit of mutual self help.

THE HULL CLUBS

The societies and guilds of the ancients are the distant ancestors of the hull clubs. The hull clubs were the forerunners of the

P & I clubs known as mutual hull underwriting associations which came into existence in the early part of the 18th century. In the hull clubs, therefore, there is a direct link between ancient and modern and many of the practices of the hull clubs and the P & I clubs find parallels with those of the guilds and many of these practices are actual derivatives of the practices of the hull clubs. A brief description of the old hull clubs is of some value, therefore, in the understanding of the workings of a modern P & I association.

Numerous accounts exist detailing the glorious history of maritime underwriting in Britain from its humble beginnings in the coffee houses of the City of London. Without detracting from such a praiseworthy past, it must be said that the traditional proprietary market of the 18th century also had a number of deficiencies and problems and it was as a reaction to these drawbacks that shipowners decided to form themselves together in mutual hull insurance associations.

Due to the unsatisfactory state of the marine insurance market there were moves, particularly by those shipowners at various outlying ports, to get together to insure their hull risks on a mutual basis. Towards the end of the 18th century there were established a number of friendly associations amongst shipowners for mutual insurance of their ships and they were particularly abundant in the north east of England especially in the coal transport trades. The North of England did not hold a monopoly in hull clubs, however, and a few associations were conducting business in London and at other ports throughout the country. Towards the middle of the 19th century there was a substantial increase in new clubs in London, some specialising in sailing vessels, iron ships, coasters and worldwide trades.

In addition to the hull clubs, there existed other classes of clubs covering other forms of risks either not covered by the traditional market or covered only at prohibitively high rates of premium. Examples of these clubs were 'cargo and freight clubs' intended for owners carrying coals and other cargoes for a shipowner's account and in respect of the owner's freight when carrying other persons' goods. These freight clubs or 'freight and outfit clubs' were there to insure a shipowner while his vessel was at sea whether carrying cargo or in ballast, because when a vessel was at sea, it required stores and outfit which was a subtraction from the freight it was earning. Other clubs were also established to indemnify members against loss caused by the customary deduction of 'thirds' and 'sixths' from the cost of new materials or repairs to their vessels. They also covered members for particular average losses on their vessels under 3% which the underwriters on the proprietary market generally did not accept. Such clubs were known as 'small damage clubs'.

Hull clubs were very local, friendly and parochial affairs usually managed only by a secretary and a manager, or in the case of the larger associations, a small committee. The manager, often a retired shipmaster, or committee decided which ships should be allowed to enter the association by arranging to survey the vessels involved. These hull clubs were local clubs and generally insured only vessels owned by the shipowners in the immediate vicinity of the clubs. They were therefore very much what can be called 'neighbourhood clubs' or local benefit societies. These friendly associations were much more than insurance companies and were much like the modern P & I associations being places where men of the sea pooled their difficulties and where help of a financial nature and otherwise was given to help sort out these problems.

The hull clubs themselves formed an immediate, local and intimate means of taking insurance on ships and indeed the personal acquaintance between members was in itself a great advantage. The members were also, generally speaking, well acquainted with the peculiarities of the area, the local ports, local weather conditions and were able to tailor their insurance requirements by means of trading areas and seasonal restrictions to fit the exact needs of the local shipowners. The system of club calls also met with the approval of shipowners as it amounted to a form of insurance on credit through payment by instalments or at least by means of deferred payments. This was unlike the proprietary insurance market which operated strictly on cash accounting. Additionally, the small hull clubs were so simple in their management and administration that they also proved very economical and being mutual in character profits did not form part of the calculations in their financing. There were, however, some disadvantages to these hull clubs. The local and parochial nature of the clubs was at first one of their great assets but as time went on it proved to be one of the greatest drawbacks to their growth and development. The club system was ideally suited to, and was developed for, a locality of a limited community of shipowners who were, of course, known to each other. Ambitious members encouraged growth so that they could boast the size of their club, and managers, wishing to increase their ad valorem remuneration, started to admit ships that were unknown to them. This development of allowing strangers to be admitted meant much of the club system began to disappear with the loss of control over entry and members lost that mutual knowledge in respect of each other's vessels. As these clubs expanded they encountered underwriting difficulties because badly maintained vessels were entered and owners of the better vessels found that they were having to pay for the losses of these inferior ships. Rating each vessel in the same amount had the effect that the good owners suffered badly when compared with the bad shipowners who indeed presented most of the claims on the club.

Further problems arose from the failure of some clubs to demand sufficiently adequate advance calls. Demanding a small advance call gave the initial impression of an economical club but the luxury of low advance calls presented problems at a later stage. The clubs, by demanding only a proportion of the total premium as an advance call and having to demand supplementary calls, made the whole underwriting arrangement a rather speculative business for both members and the club. For the members supplementary calls came as an unexpected shock, unlike the traditional system of a once and for all payment and indeed the member with claims could find that he was unable to recover his full claim from the club because of bad paying members.

As time went on the hull clubs entered a period of decline from the early 19th century. Lloyd's competed with the clubs and eventually came to offer more competitive rates. Owners of better class vessels found that they could retain better service at a cheaper price from a newly invigorated proprietary market and left the clubs which were saddled with the older badly maintained vessels that no other insurer would underwrite. This process unfortunately gave rise to the development of what became known as the 'rust-bucket clubs' which encouraged the vicious circle of poor hulls giving rise to more and more claims on smaller and smaller club funds. Many hull clubs closed during this period of the early and mid-19th century.

THE PROTECTING CLUBS

The period of decline in the hull clubs coincided with a heavy increase in liabilities imposed on shipowners in the mid-19th century. This was a period of great economic, social and technological change and a period of increase in the size, complexity and value of vessels and cargoes carried. All this accounted for a corresponding increase in the potential liability of the shipowners themselves.

Indeed, by the middle of the 19th century, shipowners found themselves faced with the threat of increasing liabilities and the Marine Insurance Act of 1745 had already prohibited shipowners from insuring against their liabilities for sums in excess of the value of their vessels.

In the year 1836 it was decided by the courts that a shipowner could not recover from his hull underwriter for damage done in a collision. This was a result of the decision in the case of *De Vaux* v. *Salvador*. The response from the traditional insurance market was to provide cover to the shipowners to the extent of only three-quarters of such expenses up to the insured value of the vessel and this left the shipowner uncovered in respect of one-fourth of the expenses, excess liability above the value of the ship, and also in respect of liabilities for death, personal injury and damage to fixed and floating objects falling outside the definition of a vessel.

A limitation of liability statute was admittedly enacted in 1845, but this statute assumed that all vessels were worth £15 per ton, whereas many ships were worth much less than this with the consequence that shipowners still found themselves paying claims in excess of the value of their own vessels.

One year after this limitation statute Lord Campbell's Fatal

Accidents Act 1846 for the first time enabled dependants to sue for damages for the death of relatives caused by the negligence of shipowners. This was at the time when British vessels were full of emigrants going to Australia and the United States of America and the consequences of this amounted, of course, to a considerable increase in potential liability.

The Fatal Accidents Act was followed a year later by a further statute, the Harbours, Docks and Piers Clauses Act 1847, which gave power to port authorities to recover for damages to port works and installations whether or not caused by negligence of the shipowner. Following this, in 1880, the Employers' Liability Act marked the first of a line of statutes providing for payment by employers, including shipowners, to workmen, including crew members, injured in the course of their employment.

It will be seen from the foregoing, therefore, the increased extent of potential liability on the shipowners of the mid-19th century and consequently they sought protection. Whilst looking for such protection shipowners found that a framework for cheap and efficient group protection already existed in the hull clubs. The system of grouping suggested itself to shipowners as the most economical means of protecting themselves against these new threats to their livelihood. Therefore, the old hull clubs were converted into 'protecting clubs' and new associations were formed in an attempt to alleviate some of the burdens being imposed on the shipowners by this increased liability. For example, the one-fourth collision liability which the proprietary insurance market would not cover was obviously a factor in the formation of the early protecting clubs. However, other potential liabilities were of equal consequence to the shipowners, particularly the liabilities arising in respect of claims for loss of life and personal injury and also for the excess liability over and above the sum insured for damage done and received in a collision.

One of the first clubs to specialise in protecting risks was a club which was inspired by Peter Tindall, an insurance broker who also managed mutual hull insurance clubs. Indeed Peter Tindall and his partners were the first to conceive the idea of a protecting club and this club, known as the Shipowners' Mutual Protection Society, commenced operations in

Topsham, Devon, on the same day as the introduction of the Merchant Shipping Act 1854, on 1 May 1855.

There were additional risks which were covered by the early protecting clubs and these arose from the rule that the amount recoverable from the insurer was limited to the value for which his vessel was insured. If the aggregate of the damage received and the damage done by the insured vessel in a collision situation, for example, exceeded the value of the insured vessel, the owner could only recover up to the insured value. It was this excess amount or 'extra risk' together with liability for loss of life and personal injury that motivated shipowners to form the early protecting clubs. However, as more and more liabilities were imposed upon shipowners so the clubs expanded to provide additional cover for those extra risks.

It was not until the latter half of the 19th century that cargo claims became a serious burden for shipowners. In 1870, for example, a vessel called the *Western Hope* was lost with her cargo off the coast of South Africa. The vessel was loaded with a cargo for Capetown but proceeded first to Port Elizabeth, thereby incurring a deviation. As a consequence of that deviation the court decided that the shipowners were not protected by the exceptions in the contract of carriage, due to the deviation being unjustifiable, and held that they were liable to pay for the full value of the cargo. The shipowner in that case was a member of the North of England Protecting Club which was not in a position to indemnify the shipowner in respect of this loss as it was a loss not contemplated by the club rules. Although the club did eventually make a small *ex gratia* payment to the shipowner, the shipowner still had to find the bulk of the settlement from his own funds.

Shortly after these unfortunate events, another vessel, the *Emily*, was lost together with her cargo following a stranding and the cargo owners recovered their full losses from the shipowner on the grounds that this was not a loss by a 'peril of the sea' but was a loss caused by negligent navigation. The forms of bills of lading commonly in use at that time were of the simplest nature and sought to protect shipowners only against the very restricted list of marine perils under common law, which do not include negligent navigation.

Obviously the shipping community was shocked by the

implications of these events and the potential liabilities to cargo interests because of losses consequent upon deviation or negligent navigation, and shipowners entered in the North of England Protection Association, therefore, suggested that an indemnity class be created, designed to cover shipowners against these additional forms of risk.

This new class of cover which was created was called 'indemnity' cover and enabled the word 'indemnity' to be added to the title of the club. In 1866 indemnity cover was commenced by the Shipowners' Mutual Protection Society and the club extended its cover under the indemnity class to include any loss, shortage or damage to cargo carried on board a member's vessel and also extended its cover to indemnify owners against fines for infringements of port, health or local by-laws or regulations.

2

WHAT IS A SHIPOWNERS' P & I CLUB?

THE NATURE AND IDENTITY OF THE MODERN P & I CLUB

Whatever may have been the earlier identity of the clubs—loose associations of shipowners with no collective rights or exposure to outside legal action—today's P & I club is quite clearly a corporation. Whereas in bygone days each aspiring member entered into a contract with the existing members, now he contracts with the corporation. This in turn provokes the thought 'should they still be called clubs?' As mere loose bandings of individuals the problem which arose was that the method by which a club was required to take legal action against one of its members was cumbersome and long-winded. An action against a member had to be taken in the individual names of all the others and in some cases a club could spend years in recovering unpaid premiums from members. Similarly, individual members encountered difficulty in bringing legal action for recovery under their contract in that they were obliged to sue each individual member for their several contributions. A club member wishing to recover from the funds of the club would have to prove the liability of all members personally since the fund was considered to be the property of all the existing members. This difficulty was compounded by the fluctuating membership of the club. Thus, incorporation was inevitable—the 'clubs' needed the simple ability to sue (and be sued) although the latter development has now exposed them to the risk of direct legal action by third parties as can be seen elsewhere in this book.

Insurance business in the United Kingdom is regulated by the Insurance Companies Act 1982 and this statute requires anyone desirous of carrying on insurance business in the UK to be either:

(a) a company, or
(b) a registered society, or
(c) a body corporate.

All the clubs now have as a result become registered companies—limited companies with no share capital (because they are essentially non-profit making and it is quite unsuitable for companies limited by shares to be other than profit making)—limitation being by guarantee to subscribe up to a specified sum in the event of the company going into liquidation. This concept of guarantee is based upon a reciprocal system, that each member is cast under a duty to refund the damages suffered by any one of them and pay, on a mutual basis, each other's claims. Furthermore, mutual members (though not members accepted as 'special entries' and who pay *fixed* premiums) undertake to contribute to the assets of the company in the case of a winding up 'such amount as may be required not exceeding a specified amount'.

The establishment of insurance companies in the United Kingdom is also controlled and governed by the Insurance Companies Act 1982 and it is a breach of that Act to carry into effect a contract of insurance without having previously sought authority to carry on insurance business. The effect of such failure and such breach of the Act is that the party who has been insured may not enforce the contract and the offending insurer is not permitted to hold on to the premium which he may have received. As to what is meant by 'carrying on insurance business', this is said to cover all aspects of the transacting of insurance business and this would include:

(a) underwriting decisions
(b) keeping accounts
(c) receipt of premium payments and
(d) notification of claims and payment of claims.

Under the equitable principles applied in the courts of the United Kingdom, however, an English commercial court judge is empowered to let a contract of insurance stand despite the fact that there may have been a technical breach of the 1982 Act provided that he, the judge, is satisfied that the insurer had genuine reason to believe that he was not acting in breach of the 1982 statute. Ironically, the Financial Services Act 1986 which, in its section 132, provides that any party who has breached the 1982 Act and who has effected a contract of insurance may not have the contract enforced against him, also states that a breach of the 1982 Act does *not* affect the validity of any *re*insurance contract in respect of the original policy.

The Marine Insurance Act 1906 in its section 85 contains a definition of mutual insurance: 'Where two or more persons mutually agree to insure each other against marine losses there is said to be a mutual insurance.' But this reflects the position prior to the incorporation of the clubs when the old hull clubs were loose associations. Liability these days falls on the club and indeed they have emphasised this legal development in their rules.

Is it correct under the modern system of incorporated P & I clubs, whereunder the prospective member enters into a contract of insurance with the corporate insurer and not with his fellow members, to continue to describe the clubs as *mutual* associations? The only justification for the word 'mutual' still to feature in the title 'mutual insurance associations' is that certainly two or more people are part of the insurance routine, that they are committed to furnish funds to pay claims for which they and/or their fellow members are liable and that all losses are dealt with thus by or with the members' money. No profits are made anyway and it is perhaps this basic point which is the single most distinctive feature which sets a club apart from a 'market' insurer. And it is in this way that it is perhaps fair to say that a member of a P & I club is not only a member but an assured *and* an insurer at the same time.

THE CONSTITUTION OF A P & I CLUB

The constitution of the club is basically laid down in the memorandum and articles of association. Apart from generally providing for the government of the club, these registered documents deal also with: who is qualified to be a member of the club; how the club may terminate a member's entry or, conversely, how a member may withdraw from the club;

liability to pay calls or contribute to the assets in the event of a winding up. Members are bound by the articles as they are when the contract of insurance is made on entry and those articles form the foundation of the contract. It has been decided that it is immaterial for the purposes of determining the liability of the parties to the contract to consider how the articles of association became the articles of the company or whether they were adopted with proper formality and any irregularity in the procedure by which the articles were altered would not detract from their binding force. This is consistent with general principles of company law. It should also be noted that a member is bound by the articles of association even if he has not seen a copy.

The supreme body of a P & I club is its general meeting which as a matter of routine is held once a year with power to convene an extraordinary meeting if any matters are so urgent as to warrant a special meeting between times.

Voting rights are usually provided for in the articles of association. Contrary to the principle whereby a member's voting power is customarily linked with the 'sum insured', the system in P & I insurance has to be different in that there is no fixed 'sum insured' so that the voting power is linked with the only other possible figure, namely the entered gross tonnage which, as will be seen, is the basis also for the premium rating and the level of calls to be calculated. In most clubs the voting is graded in order to prevent unreasonable domination by small groups of members with large tonnages. One method of grading would be to provide one vote to a member with an entered tonnage of up to 20,000 gross registered tonnes; two votes for an entered tonnage of between 20,000 and 50,000; three votes for between 50,000 and 100,000; four votes for 100,000 to 200,000 and for each extra 200,000 one extra vote. Most clubs provide in their rules that a firm of managing owners who represent several ships should not have more votes than they would otherwise have had if all the ships were owned by them. The right to vote is customarily continued to the next ordinary general meeting, even where an entered vessel is lost or missing. Entries for less than one year generally have no voting rights, but with shipowners, a period of less than one year is unusual and in any event such a limited period would be the subject of a special arrangement and this would have been agreed in advance. With charterers, the requirement of insurance for less than one year is obviously far more common and indeed many voyage charterers take out insurance for what is customarily the minimum period—two months or 1/6th of the annual premium or call. There is a necessity, of course, for fixing a minimum premium or call in this way since it would be impossible to cover the administrative costs of running an association if even the shortest haul voyages, e.g. one week, were to be charged for on the basis merely of a daily rate.

The members of a club, except those who have entered for less than one year have the entire overall conduct of that club in their hands by means of voting ability in general meetings. However, the more routine business of the association is conducted by a committee of members who are elected at the general meeting. Some clubs refer categorically to their 'committee', others to their board of directors, but these are merely alternative terms to describe the same thing. Strictly speaking, the term 'board of directors' is more technically correct since members of such committees are directors within the meaning of the Companies Act 1985. Qualifications for appointment as a 'committee man' are that they must be (a) under 70 years of age and (b) with a minimum of tonnage under his or her company's ownership actually entered in the club. As to how often the committee meets varies from club to club and could be as frequently as every month and as intermittently as only twice a year. All members of the club are eligible to sit on the committee and in a large club it would be usual to form the committee of members drawn from all categories of membership, e.g. tankers, tramps, liner vessels. It would also be customary for a third of the committee to retire in rotation and offer themselves for re-election.

Those matters which customarily come under the province of the committee are set out here in order of what would probably be considered to be descending significance:

(a) Approval of claims. Clearly the managers of any association have settlement authority for smaller value claims since it would be impossible to have the committee review every single claim regardless of size which is of concern to the association. For example, a club may allow its managers to approve settlement of up to say $50,000 any one claim. Over and above that limit, reports on each and every claim would require to be placed before the committee (at its next convenient meeting) for their prior consideration and approval before settlement can be finally made. Another club may provide that its committee has referred to it all claims over $100,000 in value but claims of that category may already have been approved beforehand by the managers and thus the committee is merely ratifying the action of the managers.

(b) Any dispute arising between a member and the club is reviewed before the committee before it goes to arbitration. Disputes between members and their club are dealt with according to the procedure defined in the club rules. Most clubs have a rule which provides as follows, or something very similar, 'if any difference or dispute between a member and the association touching any loss, claim or demand made by the member shall arise out of or in connection with these rules or any by-law thereunder, such difference or dispute shall in the first instance be referred to and adjudicated by the committee. Such reference and adjudication shall be on written submissions only.' And then a further sub-rule might read 'if the member does not accept the decision of the committee, or if the committee shall fail to make any award within three months of the reference to it, the difference or dispute shall then be referred to arbitration in London'.

After detailing the procedures for arbitration in various further subsections, a final sub-rule forbids a member to maintain any action, suit or other legal proceedings against the association otherwise than in accordance with the procedures laid down earlier in the rules and may only commence proceedings, other than the arbitration proceedings provided for, so as to enforce an award under such arbitration and then only for such sum, if any, as the award may direct to be paid by the association.

So the first stage of dispute-resolving is the committee of the club. Written submissions are to be put to them. The use of the word 'submissions' is perhaps unfortunate since it leads to a belief that the referral of the dispute to the committee is in the manner of an arbitration with the disputing parties being the member on the one hand and the club's managers, who have presumably rejected the member's claim or whatever are the issues in question, on the other hand. However, the first stage is not in the nature of an arbitration but is merely the dispassionate referral of the dispute, describing the full facts and circumstances and reason for rejection by the managers to the committee. The member himself does not usually appear before the committee nor is represented before them at that time, nor does he present his own submissions. In practical terms there is very little difference from a procedural point of view between such a referral of a dispute and the submission to the committee of a member's claim under the omnibus rule (see Chapter 4). A copy of the report to the committee of the dispute will be sent, as a matter of courtesy, to the member prior to the committee meeting but the contents are not for discussion, merely for information. If the committee rejects the member's claim, then the member may invoke the next stage of dispute resolution—namely arbitration. As has been said, each club has a sub-rule requiring members to refrain from commencing any form of litigation other than arbitration.

The sub-provision, that a member is barred from taking any form of legal action unless and until he has obtained an award in accordance with the arbitration procedure laid down in the rules, is known as the *Scott v. Avery* provision after the court case which tested its validity.

Conversely, however, in contemplating the alternative ways in which a club may take legal action against any of its individual members, e.g. to recover unpaid and overdue calls, there is always the chance to arrest a member's ship. However, in England (or Wales) this possibility is not available since the Supreme Court Act 1981 does not regard pursuit of unpaid insurance premiums as a maritime claim for which the arrest remedy lies. (Scotland, incidentally, does allow arrest for this type of claim, Scots law being independent of the law of England and Wales.) Two relevant cases on these issues found their way into the English High Court (both reported in the year 1977 in *Lloyd's Law Reports*). The first one involved the 'late' Oceanus Club which covered the plaintiffs' ships for P & I risks. A dispute arose regarding back (supplementary) and release calls. The plaintiffs eventually notified the club that they were going to proceed to arbitration as per the club's rules. Three months later the club arrested one of the plaintiffs' ships in Aruba. The High Court granted the plaintiffs an interlocutory injunction until 4.30 in the afternoon of an appointed day restraining the club first from taking any further steps in the Aruba proceedings and secondly from commencing or prosecuting proceedings otherwise than in accordance with the club's arbitration rules. The court held that the arrest action by the club was solely for the purpose of obtaining security and also that the balance of convenience favoured a refusal of the interlocutory relief since there was no suggestion that the club would not be able to satisfy any award of damages which might be made against it and that there was an obvious danger that an undertaking in damages by the plaintiffs would be worthless as the plaintiffs could dispose of their ship and distribute the assets any time they pleased, leaving nothing to satisfy the club's claim.

The second of the two cases involved the vessel *John W. Hill* which was entered for protecting and indemnity risks with the London club. Mortgagees were named as loss payee under the policy. The ship went aground up river in Venezuela and cargo had to be discharged in order to refloat her. The ship was physically damaged in the process. General average was declared but the cargo owners refused to contribute their share ($155,000). The mortgagees claimed from the P & I club. The club denied liability as they said it was not within the rules. The club applied to the United States courts (which had been invoked by the plaintiff mortgagees) for a dismissal or a stay of proceedings. The court held (1) that a contract for marine insurance was within the admiralty jurisdiction of the court; and (2) that the plaintiff mortgagees had acquired no greater rights than the assured and were bound by the conditions of the contract of insurance between the club and the member. The club's petition to stay court action was granted.

(c) Signatures on reinsurance contracts.
(d) Fixing amount and frequency of calls.
(e) Fixing of supplementary calls.
(f) Deciding on opening and closing of policy years.

(g) Remuneration for managers.
(h) Use of club's reserve funds.
(i) The application of the 'omnibus' rule to claims which are submitted for the committee's discretion.

It is in the committee system and the control exercised by the committee (of its own members) on the club's affairs that the difference between an ordinary profit making market insurance company and a mutual P & I club is most clearly demonstrated. The club is directly controlled by its own members.

It is perhaps a misconception that the benefits and obligations accruing to a P & I club member revolve around the vessel which is named as an 'entered vessel'. Quite clearly the vessel must play some part and it is indeed because of the operation of the vessel and occurrences involving the vessel that liabilities arise for her owners and thus in turn the need for insurance cover in respect of those liabilities. However, the vessel is merely the means whereby the extent of the club's liabilities is delineated. Typical wording reads as follows: 'A member shall be insured by the association against the following liabilities, costs and expenses arising in respect of his interest in the entered ship . . .'. The member as such is basically the owner of the ship in which he quite clearly has an interest but over the years the categories of persons who may apply and will be accepted for membership has widened to, e.g. charterers, operators, managers, mortgagees—even group affiliate members. Whoever these people may be, one common factor is that they must be able to show an insurable interest, which is an inescapable statutory requirement under the Marine Insurance Act 1906 (section 5):

> '(1) Subject to the provisions of this Act, every person has an insurable interest who is interested in a marine adventure.
>
> (2) In particular, a person is interested in a marine adventure where he stands in any legal or equitable relation to the adventure or to any insurable property at risk therein, in consequence of which he may benefit by the safety or due arrival of insurable property, or may be prejudiced by its loss, or by damage thereto or by the detention thereof, or may incur liability in respect thereof.'

One wonders how or why a shipbuilder or a ship repairer has an interest in a marine adventure, since a ship in dock or lying beside a repair yard is hardly engaged in an adventure, but perhaps that is covered by the extra words 'or to *any* insurable property at risk'. What really seems to be the criterion for determining the right of a person to seek membership of a P & I club is that he may be subject to the liability in respect of which he seeks protection or indemnity. Ownership itself is strictly defined (certainly in the United Kingdom) by the merchant shipping statutes. Every ship is notionally divided into 64 parts or shares. Thus owners must include co-owners, part owners, whether they be individuals or corporate persons. In one interesting old case (*Hutchinsons* v. *Wright*, 1858) the owner of 16/64ths of a ship assigned completely his shares to the party who held the balance but failed to tell his club, the Eligible Insurance Association of North Shields—a name which has long since disappeared into oblivion. The court decided that the assignment did not affect his own right to recover, which remained intact. This case was a forerunner of the modern club rule which provides that assignment of cover is outlawed unless the consent of the club is first obtained.

The entry of vessels owned on a 64th basis is usually effected by naming the managing owner or operator. For ships which are owned by 'one-ship companies' entry is effected either in the operator's name or in the name of the actual owning company. Ship charterers, who, as can be seen elsewhere in this book, may also obtain membership of a P & I club, are another class of persons with an interest in a ship to be added to shipowners, both corporate and individual, managing owners and operators. Thus, although we loosely talk about 'owners' P & I clubs', those classes of persons who may become members of a club could reasonably be contained in the following definition of 'an owner':

'In relation to an entered ship, (an owner) means an owner, owners in partnership, owners holding separate shares in generality, part owner, mortgagee, trustee, charterer, operator, manager or builder of such ship by or on behalf of whom the name has been entered in the association for insurance, whether he be a member of the association or not.'

In accordance with the constitution of the club and the club's rules, every person is considered to have agreed to become a member of the club who, in his own name or in the name of his agent or otherwise, insures any ship in pursuance of the club's memorandum and articles of association and the club's rules. In the club's rules there is generally a rule which provides that the club shall not be bound to take notice of the interest of any person, other than the members actually insuring in any ship or insurance, unless a memorandum of the name and interest of such a person has been endorsed on the certificate of entry with the consent of the club managers or of the committee of directors. It was once said by Phillimore, J (giving judgment in 1899) that 'it is very important to these associations that they should not be involved in conflict with persons other than their own members'. A little earlier than that date (in 1891 in the case of *Montgomery* v. *United Kingdom Mutual Steamship Assurance Association*), a mutual association provided in its policy that it would be liable only to members. It was held that a part owner of a ship, other than the member, could not bring an action on the policy for a loss. In the 1887 case of *United Kingdom Mutual Steamship Assurance Association* v. *Nevill* it was held that an association could not bring an action for contributions against a part owner as the undisclosed principal of the managing owner who had become a member of the club in respect of the vessel, where the club policy was expressed in a form which made only members liable upon it.

GROUP AFFILIATE MEMBERS

This expression refers to extending the benefits of club cover to companies who are affiliated to or associated with the actual member. Such action will, at the material time, be included in the certificate of entry or later evidenced thereon as appropriate.

Two provisos to the extension of benefits are (a) that recovery may be made by the affiliate/associate only if he would have been liable on the third party claim in question if he had actually stood in the shoes of the member at the time instead of where he was actually standing; and (b) that no recovery shall be paid out by the club which in aggregate (member and affiliate together) exceeds what the member would have been entitled to recover if he had faced liability alone.

MEMBERS—GENERALLY

Under P & I club rules, the owners of a ship who authorise a person to effect entry with a club and to become a member of a club are liable, as assureds, to pay the calls made by the club. The natural corollary to this proposition is that such owners should also be in a position to enforce claims against the club. Nevertheless, club rules often state that claims can be enforced only by members. Although the effect of such provisions have never arisen for decision, there are dicta which suggest that such a rule may have the effect that the owners who authorise a person to enter and thereby become 'assureds' in a club are not members. As Lord Esher said in the 1889 case of *Great Britain 100 A1 SS Insurance Association* v. *Wyllie*, 'it may be that the assured are members for the purpose of paying contributions, though not for the purpose of voting and that they are not liable to contribute to the expenses of the association other than in respect of losses of other ships insured'. Later on in the same judgment he summed up by saying, 'whether the defendants are or are not members of the association for all purposes seems to me immaterial'.

If this were in fact the position there would seem to be a stark absence of mutuality in a relationship in which for the purpose of the benefit of the club the owners are regarded as strangers, but for the purposes of the burdens they carry they are treated as members.

In a case involving the British Marine Mutual Insurance Company (1889), a policy in the Lloyd's Form was issued to the defendant's manager. He became personally liable to pay the contributions and premiums but he then became insolvent and the club sued the defendant owners as being the persons on whose behalf and for whose benefit the insurance was taken out. Bigham, J, the presiding judge, decided that the defendants, being owners of an insurable interest, were the persons for whom the insurance was effected, that there was nothing in the club's memorandum or articles of association or club rules to exclude their liability to pay the premium and the club was therefore entitled to recover. In the course of his judgment, he said:

'The association has in my opinion a double remedy: one against the member who they had permitted to enter a ship on the terms that he should be personally responsible for the contributions and another against the shipowners on whose behalf and for whose benefit the insurance has been effected.'

By entering a P & I club, a shipowner not only becomes entitled to insurance cover but he also becomes a member of the club and thereby attracts the benefit and the burdens of being a member. It is possible for an incident to occur which deprives the shipowner of his insurance cover, but his responsibilities as a member, e.g. the paying of calls, will continue. It would be near enough the truth these days to say that when a shipowner enters a club, although he is no longer strictly placed in the dual capacity of being an assured and an insurer, he does still have 'dual roles': (a) that of an assured; and (b) that of a member of the club and in these two capacities he does have distinct rights and obligations. It would also be true to say that by the entry of his name on the register of members and by the club's acceptance of his proposal, he becomes a member and his membership cannot be prejudiced or affected by there being any accident or occurrence peculiar to his case which might happen to prevent his insurance cover being effective. Conversely, in connection with the termination of membership, it is the insurance cover, not the membership, which ceases on the occurrence of prohibited activities. Thus a club whose rules contain the following wording, 'a person shall cease to be a member if for any reason whatsoever the periods of insurance of all vessels entered by him for insurance in the association shall have ended', would be as well to have a further additional protective provision to the effect that payment of calls should be the obligation not only of members but also of former members.

As Lord Alverstone, CJ, said in 1906: 'I am quite clear in my own mind that membership is something which exists for the purpose of rules independently of the actual right of a particular member to say "my ship is insured" at a particular moment'.

Because benefit of assignment (without consent) is banned it is difficult to understand why owners/charterers and/or their brokers or lawyers still persist in retaining a benefit of insurance clause in a time charter-party. The strictness of the nonassignment rule and the solid nature of the basic rule that no one other than a member may claim on the club for a loss he has suffered is illustrated by the example of a part owner (a non-member) being banned from recovery despite his co-owner being a member. Commonly the club could not bring an action to recover contributions (calls) even on the basis that the owner who was a member was at the time acting for his co-owner as an undisclosed principal.

PROCEDURE FOR JOINING A CLUB

Generally speaking, few British entries are made through brokers and most foreign entries come direct from the owners themselves, or from a club's foreign correspondents. In those few cases where a broker is used, it is the shipowner who customarily pays the brokerage and not the club.

Entry is effected by delivery to the club of an application form (a 'proposal'), the details of which will form the basis of the contract between the club and the member. Many clubs have now dispensed with the application form procedure and merely ask for the details which they require for underwriting purposes. Amongst other things a club will need to know:

(a) the applicant's hull and machinery cover;
(b) the extent of P & I cover required;
(c) the type, size and age of the vessel to be entered;
(d) the type of cargo carried in the vessel;
(e) the geographical area over which the vessel trades;
(f) the nature of the management of the vessel;
(g) the nationality of the crew;
(h) the vessel's past loss record;
(i) the flag of the vessel.

The application is considered by the club's managers who are entitled in their absolute discretion and without assigning any reason to refuse any application for entry. As soon as is practicable after accepting application, the managers must issue to the new member a certificate of entry which evidences membership in the club. This certificate is *not* a policy and does not always specify the terms of cover. It will incorporate the articles of the association by express reference and also the rules of the club which specify the risks covered. If at any time the club wishes to vary these risks against which the ship is insured, the managers will issue what is known as an 'endorsement slip' stating the date and term of such variation.

On joining a club, an owner (or interested party) takes on one burden and one benefit. The benefit: insurance cover of the scope and extent set out in the club rules. The burden: to contribute to the losses of the fellow members. This raises a curious point—supposing an incident occurs which is of the sort of gravity which would entitle the club to deprive that owner/member of his cover (for example, because of his conduct leading to or subsequent to the occurrence)—how, if at all, does it affect his obligation to continue paying contributions?

TERMINATION OF COVER

Club cover can come to an end for various reasons:

1. a member may wish to terminate of his own free will;
2. his ship may have become a total loss;
3. he may have sold his interest, whole or part, in it;
4. his entered ship may have been reported missing without trace;
5. he may have become bankrupt or gone into liquidation;
6. he simply does not or will not pay his premiums.

Clubs have an express rule laying down procedures to deal with each one of these contingencies.

A rule sometimes entitled 'termination by contractual notice' deals with 1. Both sides may terminate by the giving of written notice, the association being entitled to terminate at any time, but being obliged to give seven days' written notice to the member. The member may terminate at the beginning of the club year, i.e. at noon on 20 February, but he must give a minimum of 30 days' notice.

Termination because of 2, 3 and 4 is automatic on the happening of those events. Any alteration to such an arrangement must be agreed in writing by the club. Termination is in respect both of the contract of insurance and of the entry of the involved ship.

Inability to pay calls rather than a lack of motivation to pay is implied by 5. The event which will trigger the termination of the contract of insurance in respect of any member's interest in an entered ship is: (a) where the member is an individual person, either (1) his death, (2) a receiving order being made against him, (3) his becoming bankrupt, (4) his becoming mentally incapable of conducting his affairs; or (b) where the member is a corporate person, either (1) upon a resolution for voluntary winding up (other than for purposes of an internal reorganisation of the company or corporation), (2) upon a compulsory winding-up order, (3) upon dissolution, (4) upon the appointment of a receiver of all or part of the corporate member's business, (5) upon possession being taken by or on behalf of the holder of any debentures secured by a floating charge on any property comprised in or subject to the charge, or (6) the contract of insurance for non-payment of calls when a demand has been made for payment by the club and this has not been complied with and after notice has been served upon the member. The general effect, but this could vary between clubs, is that the club is freed from all liabilities, expenses, costs incurred, whether after *or before* the member has failed to comply with the demand for payment. The effect of this must be taken together with the general rule that a member who fails to pay his calls promptly will forfeit his right to recovery from club funds of any claim whether the origin of the claim was after or before the default in payment.

CLUB MANAGEMENT

Club management is organised in one of two ways, either by a separate firm of professional managers often as old or older established as the club itself, or by professional executives directly employed by the club itself. In the early days, in the era of small hull clubs, management duties could be carried out by a spare-time manager and a secretary. His duties were no more onerous than a part-timer could cope with. Such persons were often retired ships' masters and they were entirely suited by background and experience for such tasks. In larger clubs, small committees of members elected one of their number to the post of manager, secretary or treasurer who would carry out his duties in consideration of a small remuneration.

Functions of managers

The managerial functions are basically:

(1) handling claims
(2) underwriting
(3) investment
(4) records
(5) correspondence
(6) amendment of rules.

There are basically two established methods of dividing up the claims handling staff. The first is the syndicate method where the staff is divided into sections, each section taking care of the problems of a section of the membership, meaning whatever the type of claim that syndicate handles it. The one obvious advantage of this system is that the staff members of that syndicate get to know, on a personal basis, the members with whom they are dealing, and perhaps even more importantly, the member gets to know them. The alternative method is that the claims handling staff is divided into 'specialist' groups according to the type of claim, e.g. a cargo section, a personal injury section, an admiralty (collision, dock damage) section. The advantage of this method is that expertise in a particular type of claim is developed and deployed again to the common benefit of the membership.

One all important function of the managers is to decide who should become a member of the club which a casual observer would be forgiven for thinking was more properly the function of the committee, e.g. the members themselves deciding for themselves who they want as fellow members. It is a commonly heard remark for a senior management executive, on a PR trip to attract new members, to hear, 'Who am I getting into bed with?' For in a mutual insurance association the principle of mutuality means that after payment of advance premiums (or calls) there is a distinct possibility (probability) that a further levy may be made upon mutual members (to form a supplementary fund to make up what may have proved to be an insufficient fund made from the advance call). The likelihood of a supplementary call is influenced very much by the quality of the members and the high, or otherwise, standards of their operations.

The managers are also responsible for the selection and supervision of a network of correspondents worldwide and the high standard and efficiency of this network is the very foundation of the service provided by the club to its members. As to whether the clubs should, generally speaking, have legal or commercial correspondents is a matter of opinion. Clearly claims handling is very substantially legal work but there are many routine duties which a club correspondent should perform which would 'neither stretch the legal mind' nor justify the charging of a fee on a professional law scale, e.g. the appointing of a cargo damage surveyor, or merely attending on board to render assistance to the master or deal with the disembarkation of a stowaway.

Some clubs compromise by maintaining both a legal and a commercial representative in a particular port. In the USA traditionally it seems, all club representatives (with the exception of New York only) are firms of attorneys.

Service on a global basis is vital to the efficient operation of any P & I club and all clubs, both with large tonnages and small, have established a network of correspondents (or 'representatives') familiar with P & I matters in all significant ports of the world. The first significant appointment of an overseas correspondent by a British-based club was that of Captain Langlois, a ship's master, appointed by the Britannia Club in Antwerp and indeed the company which the captain formed and which still bears his name is very active in Belgium to this day representing many of the major clubs. Club managers are very careful not to use the word 'agent' when referring to their correspondents around the world since the former word tends to imply that the clubs could be said to be doing business in the particular foreign territory where the agent is situated and where he is operating. The risks attendant on the doing of business are particularly high in the United States where certain maritime territories do have direct action statutes enabling local citizens to take action directly against insurers and the clubs are keen not to be seen to be doing anything which might convince a local judge that they were doing business in or had assets in the territory concerned. An added advantage of not regarding correspondents as agents or referring to them as agents is that they cannot be authorised to accept service of process or themselves submit to the jurisdiction on behalf of the club. The State of Louisiana is perhaps the most 'dangerous' state in the United States so far as foreign-based clubs are concerned since it does have a direct action statute and it is frequent that the name of one of the European-based clubs appears as second defendant on a writ which is primarily taken out against a shipowner member. In the case of *The 'Vainqueur Jose'* (referred to on page 129) it was found that a law firm in New York, which were listed correspondents of a P & I club, were not competent to accept notice of a potential claim from a member of the club in regard to the latter's duty to give notice of claims under the club rules. The duty to give notice is one of the paramount rules and should be given as soon as possible after any occurrence which might give rise to a claim. Failure to notify in that way does give the club's committee discretion to reject or reduce the claim.

The amount of authority which a club will extend to its correspondent to act on its own initiative varies but generally speaking correspondents will be allowed to handle and authorise settlement of small claims up to a certain fixed maximum but claims exceeding such a maximum are expected to be referred to the club's headquarters for further authority. Masters of ships should be informed who their club's representatives are and this can be done by equipping them with a current copy of the club's list of worldwide representatives. This is probably one of the greatest features of a club's service to its members that their ships' masters may call in the club's local representative in any particular port if a problem has arisen of a P & I (or even defence) nature upon which he requires advice or assistance. Quite often a club's representative will be not so much of a claims handler but a 'go-between' or 'smoother-over' of problems between a ship's master or ship's agent and local port officials, such as immigration or Customs officers, police or harbour authorities. Ideally, perhaps, each club should have a legal and a commercial representative in each port, though in practice this is not done and in only a verv few ports are both types of representatives to be found in one port. In the United States, as has already been mentioned, all club correspondents tend to be law firms with the exception of New York, where Lamorte Burns and Company take care of a large part of the P & I work. So far as legal advice in New York is concerned it is very much a 'free market' and there are many firms of lawyers well versed in maritime and admiralty law who are available to take on legal work for shipowners or charterers.

OFF-SHORE ASSOCIATIONS

Many of the British clubs have 'gone off-shore', an expression which leaves the casual observer to assume that they are seeking tax advantages. This has an element of truth in it. Bermuda, for example, does grant 'exempt' status which means that investment income and capital appreciation are free from taxation. It is important to remember that the income derived from calls is used very largely for the payment of claims and those claims are paid in all manner of different currencies. In the old days when clubs were headquartered in the UK, funds held in Britain had to be held in sterling. As and when sterling lost value against other currencies, the clubs would stand to lose perhaps millions of pounds and this could only be recouped by a levy on members of supplementary calls, unacceptable at the best of times. As the clubs became more and more international in their membership the British laws, taxation and financial restrictions, became more and more disadvantageous. However, the British Government could not be persuaded to relax its laws for the benefit of these international clubs. So arose the incentive to move 'off-shore'. Clubs sought a country which allowed funds to be held in a number of different currencies so as to offset losses due to currency fluctuations. Generally, managers have been established in order to manage the new overseas clubs with the old London managers being retained as London agent.

The effect of moving abroad is that funds in whatever currency can be held without fear of erosion and can be changed into whatever currency is necessary to effect timely and amicable claims settlements. Administratively, as opposed to financially, there is little difference between a Bermuda-based or Luxembourg-based and a London-based club. The underwriting and claims work continues to be performed in London by managing agents. Equally importantly, the law governing the relationship between club and members has remained English and no attempt was made to incorporate the law of the particular 'off-shore' country.

Some clubs have persisted in allegiance to the UK but have been persuaded nevertheless of the wisdom of alleviating the burden of tax on investment income and thus have formed reinsurance subsidiaries in off-shore territories.

The policy of moving off-shore is thus basically a cushioning process against the eroding effects of inflation, devaluation and/or drastic fluctuation in the rates of exchange. That UK investment taxation was also in the mind's eye must be regarded as an additional natural fear.

Inflation
Revaluation
Exchange Rate fluctuations.

3

UNDERWRITING AND CALLS

Underwriting in general is the subject of a great deal of mystery and complexity and generally the underwriting for P & I risks is more complicated than for normal hull or cargo insurance business.

There always remains the element of uncertainty as to the nature of possible liability claims because until the situation related to a claim becomes clear the amounts involved cannot be definitely established. By comparison with ordinary hull or cargo insurance the assured is required to pay a premium for the exact value of the subject matter at risk under the insurance policy and that value will be the extent of an assured's possible exposure to liability. In the field of P & I insurance this is not ascertainable and therefore cannot be so readily quantified.

Protection and indemnity underwriters have, however, become so expert in the art of predicting the unpredictable that P & I clubs have branched out into insuring other risks, such as strikes, freight, demurrage and defence, loss of hire, which the traditional marine insurance market has tended to avoid. This has led in recent times to even further diversification by the clubs to insure risks arising from professional indemnity and negligence on a mutual basis.

Historically, the protection and indemnity associations have, for the most part, restricted themselves to covering shipowners' liabilities on vessels. This exercise of underwriting ships entered in the clubs is carried out once a year in relation to each policy year of insurance. Customarily, the policy year starts on 20 February and continues for one complete year. This attachment date is normally common to all members in the clubs and is necessary in this form because the club or mutual call system is not based on a fixed premium underwriting basis and therefore if the claims paid or outstanding exceed the initial call made on the members of the club in any particular year, then the members for that year must make good the deficit by paying a supplementary call. For such a system to be viable it is essential that the members and the ships insured in any given year be readily ascertainable and this is only achieved by having a common date of attachment. It is true to say that in recent years there has been a certain amount of primary, as opposed to reinsurance or excess P & I, insurance being offered to the traditional market. However, primary P & I insurance is not popular with the traditional market and has consequently never been successfully written. This attitude is borne out by the fact that some 90% of the world's gross registered tonnage obtains its P & I insurance cover through entry into one of the traditional P & I associations that make up the international group of P & I associations.

It may be possible to explain the reluctance on the part of the traditional market underwriters to accept P & I risks by explaining that the traditional marine market operates a system of 'fixed' or 'once and for all' premiums, a system that is not ideally suited to the vagaries of P & I business.

Under the scheme where single premiums are charged by underwriters, the underwriters themselves tend to err on the side of caution by setting premiums which may be unattractive, or alternatively, where the premium may be set at too low a rate, one catastrophic claim can lead to serious losses for the underwriter. Under this system of fixed premiums, underwriters are unable to go back to their assured and ask for more premium when claims are excessive.

To overcome this very unpredictable situation for third-party liabilities the mutual clubs do have the possibility of seeing how things develop and as necessary, should the catastrophe happen, spread the cost of that large claim throughout the membership of the club by means of imposing supplementary calls.

The second aspect which proves unattractive to the traditional market underwriters is their reluctance to become involved in long-drawn-out negotiations on claims that quite regularly lead to litigation. In the P & I associations the claims handling services of the clubs are a vital element in the service and coverage that they provide. Not only is this claims handling service a great attraction to the individual member, who has an outstanding claim against him, but is a great beneficial service to the whole of the membership of the club as it contributes to reducing the size and number of claims that may be made on the association and can in turn lead to levels of calls being kept to a minimum.

A third aspect of this situation is that the traditional marine market underwriters prefer to know as soon as conceivably possible the extent of claims so that they can assess losses or indeed profits. However, this situation does not prevail in P & I insurance as inevitably the making of claims, the subsequent negotiation and possible settlement can take a considerable period of time and it is not unusual for a club to have to wait three, four, five or more years before being in a position to say whether any individual club year has been successful or otherwise.

THE HISTORY OF MUTUAL RATING

Most of the P & I associations were formed when the business of their members was being conducted on a national rather than on an international basis. Owners were in the main operating comparable vessels in comparable trades under their national flag and were consequently exposed to comparabilities which they were unable to insure in the conventional insurance markets. As a result, because all members needed coverage on the same basic terms, against the same basic liabilities to which they were all equally exposed, it was clearly equitable that each member should contribute the same rate of premium or call to create the fund out of which claims would be paid. This became known as the 'standard rate' and was payable on the gross registered tonnage of the entered ship with no apparent adjustment being made for good or bad records, it being considered that each member was equally exposed to the risk and, therefore, it was purely a matter of good fortune how the claims may have ultimately fallen.

There was, therefore, during this period, equality of risk and of contributions, which indeed is the concept of mutuality in its purest sense, with an association of shipowners joined in a common aim of self protection. This system, however, had its unfortunate effects in that good, careful shipowners with efficient and well structured and managed vessels were in effect bled by owners of badly maintained vessels because of the number of claims instigated by inefficient, badly maintained ships.

Whilst in those early days the constitution of the United Kingdom associations was mainly British flag tonnage, gradually the success of the clubs began to attract foreign shipowners whose exposure to risk was similar although not necessarily identical to that of the original members. This aspect was particularly prevalent when the hull insurances were arranged in markets outside London and the terms of the coverage included some of the risks which would otherwise have been covered by the P & I associations. Gradually the ships operated by owners were becoming more and more varied in type, size and sophistication of their equipment and more diverse in the nature of their trading and the cargoes that they carried. Therefore, the equality of risks that had been based on equality of contribution was gradually changing and in so doing it became evident that some revision of the principle of a common rate of contribution based on the tonnage of the vessel was necessary in order to achieve a fair distribution of risk and cost quite plainly based on mutuality among the members.

This led to systems being developed which took greater account of the individual characteristics and requirements of the shipowner and ensured that a more sophisticated method of individual underwriting was designed to see, as far as possible, that one group of members was not being subsidised by the other. Some associations adopted a complex system of rebates, bonuses and surcharges based on each member's individual characteristics and requirements according to the nature of the trade, cargoes, type of ships, flag, type of operation or standard of management.

This type of rating was maintained for a considerable number of years and it proved during that time, in general, to have the flexibility necessary to maintain equality amongst the membership. A minor amendment was required, however, due to the application of the surcharge or rebate to a standard rate of call, which indeed sometimes resulted in the actual rate of call being expressed in awkward fractions of currency. Therefore, in the 1950s the method was changed so that a percentage surcharge or rebate was applied instead to the gross registered tonnage of the vessel entered in the club, and not the standard rate as prevailed previously. This in effect produced a 'contributing tonnage' and the result of this was identical since the call to be paid was calculated by multiplying the contributing tonnage by the standard rate of call. This system unfortunately had undesirable side effects which developed with owners operating many various types of ships in as many various types of trades and some shipowners varied the terms of their coverage from the basic terms offered by the association by means of deductibles or because they carried certain of the risks themselves. These wide variations in terms therefore resulted in a wide variation in premiums so that the concept of the 'standard rate' of call became unmanageable and meaningless.

These developments led to the 'contributing tonnage system', which was later abandoned in favour of the adoption of the 'premium rating system' which achieves the same result in a much simplified way, whereby each vessel is individually assessed at a premium rating per gross registered ton, which is based on the exposure to risk involved with that particular member.

THE COST TO EACH MEMBER

Each individual member of a P & I association will be quoted his own individual premium rating, reflecting the risks against which he wishes to be covered and the potential exposure to risk being accepted by the individual club in respect of his vessels.

It is quite normal for the advance call to be 100% of the premium rating, although this is flexible amongst many of the clubs.

When giving consideration to any member's rating the club underwriters will first take into account the cost per ton of the excess reinsurance, the anticipated contributions to the international pooling agreement (these aspects are referred to elsewhere) and the general administration expenses. This total of items is added to by a further calculation being referred to as retained premium which represents that part of the premium available to meet claims, which it is expected will be brought on the association before the pooling agreement and the excess reinsurance are involved.

In an ideal situation this proportion of premium received from any one of the members will equal the claims arising from that member's ships in the ensuing year, that is, below the point at which the pooling agreement would take over. It is the constant aim of the club's underwriters at each renewal to adjust the members' premium rating. In order that this aim can be achieved the proportion which each member's retained premium bears to his total calls is regarded as his acceptable loss ratio. This will be referred to later on in this chapter.

RENEWALS

The exercise of underwriting ships entered with a particular association is carried out once a year in relation to each policy year of insurance. The policy year starts on 20 February and continues until 20 February the following year.

There is no particular magic in this date, but as it differs from the normal market policy year of 1 January to 1 January, it deserves a little explanation. 20 February was traditionally the date when the ice in the Baltic Sea started to break up and allow freedom of movement to vessels engaged in sea trade and thus the time for maritime accidents (the subject matter of P & I insurance) to start happening.

Therefore, it is the task of the club underwriters to adjust the premium rating for each member so that it fairly reflects the risk to the club of claims from that member during the ensuing year. They will take into account the call and claims record of the member over previous years, comparing his loss ratio with his acceptable loss ratio after making any allowances for recoveries from the pool or the excess reinsurance. They will allow for any changes over the past years in the cover which the member has selected and also any adjustments which may have been made to his premium rating over recent renewals.

The underwriters will also consider any particular factors which may help them to make a fair assessment, such as any changes in the trade of the vessels concerned, the development of improving or worsening trends in the member's loss record, or the fact that otherwise a good loss record is spoilt by a single heavy claim.

Where a member of the club, or a group of associate members, has a number of ships entered in the club, it may be in the best interests to group those various ships' calls and claims records together and as a result of this greater spread of premiums, the effect will be to cushion the occasional heavy claim on the record, so the club underwriters can generally allow a lower average premium rating than would be needed for a single ship entry. However, any member can always elect to have each ship rated individually if he so wishes. Obviously, the club underwriter will do all he can to arrive at a fair premium rating assessment for each member at each renewal. Ideally each member's loss record would always be in balance, but since these claims can never be entirely predictable his loss ratio will inevitably fluctuate either side of this ideal level. Further, as each member of the club is contributing his share of the pool and reinsurance costs, any member who has lower claims than envisaged within the retained layer will be contributing that year to support those whose claims may have been higher than expected. However, the reverse position could occur in the following year and in this way a member will be given the full benefits of mutuality.

INFORMATION REQUIRED BY UNDERWRITERS

We can now ask, how is the premium rate arrived at? If anyone who has not previously been insured with the club asks for a rate to be quoted for his ship or ships, a considerable number of important factors have to be given consideration in the underwriting process.

In addition to the details required from members on entry for the purposes of the club's membership records, members will also be required to furnish more detailed information to enable the club's underwriter to assess the level of premiums.

The basic considerations for underwriting in order to assess the risk involved in accordance with the requirements for cover of the prospective member include the following.

1. First there is the nature and extent of existing insurance cover, particularly with regard to the member's hull and machinery insurance. The club underwriters will need to be aware of such coverage as, for example, the prospective member may be insured under hull conditions covering 4/4ths collision liability in which case an amount may have to be deducted from the member's premium in order to reflect the reduced exposure of the club compared to its exposure if the member had required 1/4th collision liability insurance cover from the club.

2. The club also may require knowledge of the nature and size of deductibles being carried by a member under other insurances which could cause a corresponding increase in the exposure of the club.

3. The prospective member must state whether cover is likely to be required to include or exclude cargo liabilities, passenger liabilities and/or crew liabilities.

4. Additionally, the club will need to know the nationality of the crew, particularly with regard to the availability of state social welfare insurance and special contractual obligations. The nationality of the crew of an entered vessel is, of course, highly relevant because of the exposure of the owner to claims arising out of injuries, loss of life, redundancy and repatriation which will vary from one nationality to another because of varying state regulations. There may be unusual contractual obligations which a member has entered into with his crew or crew supplier and the club will wish to consider these and may approve them only on the condition that the member's call rate and terms of entry are adjusted accordingly.

5. Full details of the type of vessel or vessels to be entered in the club will be required by the underwriter, for example, details of its type, flag, age, size, design and class are all factors which will clearly affect the exposure of the member and in turn the club to the various risks.

6. The areas the ships are likely to be trading and the

types of trade that the vessel will undertake are of extreme importance and the underwriter will be concerned with the types of cargoes to be carried, whether passengers will be carried, geographical trading pattern routes and periods of the year when trading will take place. The type of cargo is of great importance as, for example, a bulk carrier employed in the carriage of ore is likely to have a better claims record than a bulk carrier carrying a more delicate type of cargo. The vessel's geographical operations are significant because, for example, vessels trading to the United States are potentially exposed to a worse claims record in respect of certain claims such as 'longshoreman's' injury claims. Details of any long-term charter commitments and the terms and conditions of such contracts will be taken into consideration.

7. The quality of the vessel's management will have a great influence and the underwriter will require to be informed of the experience of the vessel's management, the level of crew training and evidence of the ship's continuing maintenance.

8. The vessel's previous claims record will be examined over as long a period as is available and usually for at least the previous five years.

ACCEPTABLE LOSS RATIO

We have already seen that when an owner has insured his ships with the particular club for a number of years, his rate for each year will largely be determined by his claims record over the previous years. This way a complete record for that particular manager and his fleet is produced in order to show his record, policy year by policy year, to include:

1. The tonnage entered.
2. The calls that have been paid.
3. The claims that have been paid and those that are on an estimated basis (to be known as outstanding claims not yet settled).
4. The loss ratio, which is a figure arrived at by dividing the claims by the premium figures.

Put in a simple way, this overall record will show the claims which may be expected from the ships and what premiums have actually been paid. On a very broad basis it might therefore be said that if the experience shows that the claims are in excess of the premiums, the shipowner can expect to pay an increase in the rate and the opposite is true if the premiums are in excess of the claims—a possible reduction.

However, from a practical point of view the underwriting of any ship or fleet is considerably more sophisticated. For example, when looking at the actual loss ratio the underwriters will compare that figure with the acceptable loss ratio for any particular member. The acceptable loss ratio is calculated by subtracting from the total calls paid by the member the costs which the club has to pay for that member's share of excess reinsurance, pool claims and administration. For example, a shipowner with a low premium rate will have a lower acceptable loss ratio than a shipowner with a high premium rate. Further attention has to be paid to adjustments in rate in previous years and whether during the years to which the record relates, there have been any changes in the member's cover. At each renewal the underwriters, therefore, attempt to adjust the premium rating for each member so that the premium it produces reflects the risks that the member brings to the association.

With regard to remarks made on acceptable loss ratio the member who enjoys a low premium rating, say, because of high deductibles or restrictive cover will have a lower acceptable loss ratio than a member who because of full cover and low deductibles is rated higher. The former pays a smaller total by way of calls and therefore a larger percentage of this call has to be paid by the association in respect of reinsurance. This is because the reinsurance contract is on a tonnage as opposed to a premium basis and the effect of this is that the acceptable loss ratio can vary between 20% and 70% of the overall account.

At each renewal the underwriters will attempt to make adjustments to the premium rating for each member so that it is commensurate with the risk to the association that has been created by the member. Any changes that are made in the nature of trade of the ships concerned will, of course, be taken into account as also will the referred comparison between the actual loss ratio of the member, after allowing for any recoveries from the pool or the excess reinsurances and his acceptable loss ratio. When one examines these loss ratios it is relevant to know and to allow for any changes which may have taken place over the past years in the coverage which the member enjoys and also any adjustments up or down which may have been made to his premium rating over recent renewals.

In a strict sense underwriting is not an exact science, but a science that has been described as 'arranged and organised common sense', and, by another, as 'organised knowledge'. In this sense then P & I underwriting is a science and every endeavour is made to practise it in a scientific manner. Club underwriters will use their best endeavours within the framework of the principles set out above to arrive at a fair premium rating assessment at each renewal, attempting to achieve the perfect result where each member who contributes his proportionate share to the pool, excess reinsurance and administration costs for some amount equal to his total claims below the point where the pooling agreement takes over. It would, of course, be very unusual for such a result to be achieved for any member year after year because undoubtedly the loss ratio will fall below the acceptable loss ratio figure in some years and in others it will rise above it. However, the constant aim is to reach the point where it will maintain an acceptable level whereby in effect what is happening is that each member is contributing his due share of the pool and reinsurance costs and in any year those members whose claims have been small will have contributed towards the cost of those members whose claims are higher.

CALLS

One of the distinctive features of P & I club insurance directly relating to the underwriting function and virtually the main feature central to the concept of mutuality is the system of levying calls rather than charging premiums. On this subject, section 85(2) of the Marine Insurance Act 1906 states: 'The provisions of the Act relating to the premium do not apply to mutual insurance, but a guarantee, or such other arrangements as may be agreed upon, may be substituted for the premium.'

It has been said that calls are 'equivalent to the premium' but it is probably a more accurate description to refer to calls as merely bearing a 'family likeness to premiums'. It is the case that the premium is the price for which an insurer undertakes his liabilities whereas in the case of P & I associations this price is a consideration rather than an actual payment, it consists, instead, of an agreement by a member to become liable to contribute to the losses of other members of the club. The price that the member pays for his insurance with the P & I association is not calls or the sums of money he actually pays but it is his undertaking to be liable to pay calls in the manner provided by the rules of the association to the losses of himself and other members and to the expenses of management, investments and reinsurance premiums.

P & I club rules would normally provide that members shall contribute by way of calls all funds which in the opinion of the committee are required to meet the general expenses of the club. These are to meet the claims, expenses and other outgoings, whether incurred, accrued or anticipated, of the insurance business of the club in respect of any such policy year, including any proportion of any claims or expenses of any insurer other than the club, which has fallen or which may be thought likely to fall on the club by virtue of any reinsurance or pooling agreement concluded between the club or such other insurer.

Funds that have been raised by way of calls may also be diverted towards other general reserves, to 'catastrophe funds' or otherwise as the committee may consider expedient.

PREMIUM RATING, ADVANCE AND SUPPLEMENTARY CALLS

In the early hull and protecting clubs calls were made upon members for each single claim and where no claims were made upon the club then no calls were made. This was considered possible at the time because of the small number of entries and very small cost of administration. Therefore although with a large number of entries, or potentially high number of claims and higher costs of administration, such a system would be impossible, one fact has not changed and that is that the clubs still underwrite 'at cost' in that there is no element of profit included in the computation of calls.

The basic equation for underwriting is that calls plus investment income should equal claims plus expenses plus reinsurance premiums. When calculating the size of calls the club needs to consider the call income required to cover a member's claims within the club's own retention, a contribution to claims, a proportion of the excess reinsurance premium, together with management expenses and investments.

The basic rate achieved by weighing these factors which the underwriter would have collected will be multiplied by the contributing or gross tonnage for the period of cover and this will produce the rate of advance call.

When considering the advance call the club directors will, before the beginning of each policy year, decide what proportion of the total anticipated call income for the year they wish to call in advance. This advance call is usually payable in two, or sometimes more, instalments throughout the year depending on the individual club policy.

The club's rules will generally provide that the committee of directors may decide, during the course of a policy year, that for the next policy year the contributions of the vessels entered into the club should generally be increased.

From all the information gathered by the underwriting department the managers of the association will calculate a total call to be paid by each member in respect of his period of entry. The advance call rate per ton is then calculated depending on the proportion of the total bill that is payable as an advance call in the policy year. Clubs may well call 100% in advance with an indication of a supplementary call or may call 80% in advance leaving approximately 20% for any anticipated supplementary call.

Club rules generally give power to the association to levy supplementary or additional calls and it is normal for the committee or the managers to indicate an estimate of the percentage at which it is hoped that any supplementary call or calls will be levied. However, it is made abundantly clear by the club rules that any such estimate for supplementary calls shall be entirely without prejudice to the right of the committee or managers to levy supplementary calls at a greater or lesser percentage than that indicated and the club will further disclaim any liability whatsoever arising as a result of any estimate or in respect of 'error, omission or inaccuracy' contained in that supplementary call estimate.

It is important when comparing call rates from one club to another that important factors, such as accuracy of estimating total calls, are taken into consideration. Except for possible cash flow benefits to the members it should realistically make no difference whether a club calls in 10% or 90% of its estimated total advance call. What is more crucial to members is whether the club is able to keep accurately to its stated estimate of the total call.

An advance rate may appear cheap on the basis of the club's supplementary call estimates but it may transpire to be substantially more expensive than the member had been led to believe. It could be argued that high advance calls take money out of the pockets of the members, which could be usefully employed in their business, a so-called 'insurance on credit'. Alternatively, it may be said that the fund from large advance calls could be used by the club for investments which will earn interest and which will go some way towards reducing the size of supplementary calls levied. From the clubs' viewpoint high advance calls also obviously reduce the risk of bad debts when supplementary calls are levied.

Hi Call — Less bad debt.

CLUB FUNDS

Most clubs provide the committee or board of directors with wide discretion as to how funds are to be disposed of. For example, if any funds shall have been pooled and invested, the committee may apportion as they think fit the income arising on the pooled investments among and between different policy years, reserves and accounts from which the fund or funds so invested originated.

Similarly, club rules may also contain provisions for the establishment of reserve funds and the purposes for which those reserves may be utilised. The club committee or board of directors may establish and maintain such reserve funds or other accounts for contingencies as they deem fit. Such funds are established and maintained to provide a source of funds which may be applied for any general purposes of the association, including the need to stabilise the level of additional calls and to eliminate or reduce the need to levy additional calls in respect of any particular policy year. They may be used to eliminate or reduce a deficiency which has occurred or which is thought likely to occur in respect of any closed policy year and they may protect the association against any actual or potential losses on exchange rates or in connection with its investments.

The funds necessary to establish these reserves or other contingency type accounts can be raised by the committee or board of directors when deciding on the rate of any advance or additional calls for any particular policy year. They may resolve that any specified amount or proportion of such calls may be transferred to and applied for the purpose of any such account.

Also, the committee, on the closing of any policy year or at any time thereafter, may resolve that any specified proportion of funds standing to the credit of that particular policy year can be transferred once again to a reserve or contingency fund. Consequently, if at any time after the closing of a particular year it appears to the committee or board of directors that the claims, expenses and outgoings arising in respect of that policy year may exceed the total amount of calls and other receipts for the year, then the deficiency can be accounted for by transferring funds from the reserve or contingency accounts to assist that particular closed policy year.

Transferring excess calls to a particular deficient policy year, if applicable to the entire membership, can, in those circumstances, be a breach of mutuality in that it is asking members of, for example, the 1988/89 policy year to pay for the losses of the membership of an earlier year. However, members do agree to such liability by confirming that, as members who have entered vessels for insurance in the association in respect of any policy year, they shall provide by way of calls to be levied all funds which in the opinion of the committee are required. That is, for such transfers to be made as the committee may direct and think proper to meet any deficiency which has occurred or may be thought likely to occur in any closed policy year.

In view of the fact that members of a particular accounting period are required to cover a deficit due to the reserves of previous years being insufficient, they should also have the benefit of distributing amongst themselves any surplus earned by reserves in previous years. Obviously, such a practice will breach the principle of mutuality which lies behind the whole reason for having a fixed policy year, that is each year should stand on its own feet and pay for itself and that all members of the club can be defined and ascertained for a definite period of time. It would not be equitable to distribute surpluses to members for the accounting year in which the excess reserves happen to be credited to the accounts. Some clubs, therefore, provide that only surpluses which are mainly due to good results in the course of the accounting year shall be distributed to members of that year.

Some clubs provide in their articles of association that the surpluses that are not distributed shall be allocated to a reserve fund and go on to provide that such a reserve fund may not be applied to reduce the contribution in future years if such contribution is due to the results of the year, but may be applied to make up for insufficient reserves in previous years.

Responsibility for investment is generally placed with the board of directors who have responsibility for the investment of any contingency account, catastrophe reserve fund and general reserves. Because of the complexities of investment policies, the directors, almost universally, employ professionally qualified investment managers and merchant bank advisers.

The combination of calling in a relatively large amount of funds in advance calls and the long 'tail-back' inherent in the settlement of P & I insurance claims means that the clubs have large funds available for investment. Such funds, however, together with the various 'buffer' funds, of course, are held not to earn profits for distribution but in order eventually to settle claims and the clubs arrange their investment portfolios accordingly.

Those clubs which have gone 'off-shore' have taken advantage of overseas fiscal attractions by various means. Some clubs have wholly-owned off-shore subsidiaries with whom they enter into reinsurance arrangements. As these funds are really balances available for outstanding claims they are invested in such a way as to remain stable for the payment of claims and a low risk policy of investment is generally pursued in order to protect the capital. Further, investments must be marketable in order to be realised when necessary for the rapid settlement of claims. Most funds held by clubs are spread in roughly the same proportion to match approximately the underlying frequency of the claims with the funds within the association's reserves. The freedom from exchange control has been of great assistance in this policy.

THE 'CLOSING' OF POLICY YEAR

In order to underwrite on a mutual basis at all it is essential that each member's record is looked at, at the same time and for the same period.

In respect of each member's records there is noted an estimate of the number and size of claims. In this way a policy year can be closed even though claims are still outstanding because all claims will have at least been notified and estimated. It is therefore quite possible to close a policy year without having every claim presented and paid for. The rules of P & I associations provide for this where the committee may declare that any policy year is closed notwithstanding that it is known or anticipated that there are in existence, or may be in the future, claims, expenses or other outgoings in respect of that policy year which have not yet accrued or where the exact amounts have not yet been established.

Most P & I club rules contain provisions which will state when a policy year is closed and the club is no longer entitled to make any more supplementary calls from its members.

In some cases club rules will provide that no 'catastrophic calls' can be levied after the close of the particular policy year. For this very reason it is imperative that the claims departments within P & I associations are extremely careful when preparing their estimates of outstanding claims in order that the clubs can maintain sufficient reserves to pay for any 'surprise claims' which may arise.

The period of time for any policy year to be kept open varies from association to association and indeed from year to year. Some clubs' policy years can conceivably be closed after sometime between 15 months to four years and any such decision as to when it would be expedient to close a particular policy year is generally left to the discretion of the committee or directors of the particular P & I club.

SURPLUSES

After a particular policy year has come to an end the club will take account of income that has been derived from the advance call and the expenditure of claims settled and outstanding together with other related expenses. Any excess of expenditure over income is then collected from the members by means of a supplementary call or calls which are calculated in proportion to the members' advance calls. If income exceeds expenditure, however, a return can be made to the member or alternatively invested in various funds held by the association. It will be seen that clubs provide unlimited liability cover to their members and, therefore, it is logical that a member's liability for additional or supplementary calls is based on the experience of the club as a whole and takes no account of the claims record of the individual members during the policy year then current. Any surpluses sufficient to make a return to the members are quite rare with most clubs, although clubs do provide for the possibility of making rateable returns to members either by powers given to them in the articles of association or in the club rules.

When a policy year is closed and the balance sheet shows a surplus, such a surplus can be dealt with, according to the rules of the club, in a variety of ways. As has already been noted most clubs provide themselves with the power to make returns to the members and the club rules contain provisions which provide for dealing with underwriting surpluses. In some instances a club's rules will provide that if upon the closing of any policy year it appears to the committee that any part of the calls and other receipts in respect of the said policy year is unlikely to be required to meet the claims, expenses and outgoings arising from that particular policy year, then the committee may well decide to dispose of any excess which in their opinion is not required in one of the following ways:

(a) By transferring the excess or any part thereof to the reserves of the association.
(b) By applying the referred excess to meet any deficiency which may have occurred or is thought likely to occur in any closed policy year.
(c) By returning the excess or any part thereof to the members who were entered into the association for the particular policy year.

The problems, therefore, in closing policy years and indeed for the consideration of renewals in underwriting arise clearly because of the long 'tail-back' of claims and settlements and it is often several years before it is possible to settle a member's most recent claims record. At the time of any particular renewal it is most unlikely that the figures for the current year will at the time be sufficiently developed to give any guide for the future. The result of this is that changes in a member's premium rating, whether up or down, tend to lag some three years behind the changes in claims trends. Generally, if a member is concerned that his rating by the managers of the association is unfair, he has the right to submit a case to the committee or the directors for consideration. For this reason the clubs, unlike traditional hull and machinery underwriters, do not look at the most recent claims record because, as P & I claims take so long to settle, it is difficult for a meaningful claims record to emerge without examining a claims record of perhaps three, four or even more years.

In the case of *Volkswagenwerk A.G. and Wolfsburger Transport Gesellschaft mbH* v. *International Mutual Strike Assurance Company (Bermuda)*, it was contended by a member of the association that a club rule which provides that if at the end of the policy year the vessel continued to be entered in the club its entry will continue on the same terms as before. The word 'terms' included the amount of its advance calls. The court decided that such construction of this club rule, which would have the effect that advance calls would remain immutable and unalterable, was a nonsense.

CLUB RESERVES

When P & I associations have collected their calls from their members it is the task of the association to ensure that these funds are preserved and made available to pay necessary claims and expenses of the member.

The management of these funds which have been collected by the club and subsequent decisions as to how these funds are to be managed and indeed how to deal with any surpluses and investment policy, are generally in the hands of the committee or the directors.

The income and expenditure accounts of P & I associations are similar to profit and loss accounts of any insurance company. There is some difference, however, and that is, that the income side of the accounts, including income from investments and interest, is relatively high. The reason for this is due to the investment of revenues for outstanding claims which is much larger in the case of a P & I association than its comparable non-life insurance company. This is due to the fact that there are more litigious claims involving lengthy claims settlement processes and consequently there can be few claims paid in the same year that the losses actually arise.

The majority of clubs have rules which provide the committee with very wide powers related to investment of income. It is quite normal, for example, that the funds of a particular association may be invested under the direction of the committee or the board of directors by means of the purchase of stocks, shares, bonds, debentures or other securities or the purchase of currencies, commodities, or other real or personal property or can be invested by means of depositing in such accounts or by being loaned on such terms and in such a manner as the committee may think appropriate. The committee may also direct that all or any of the funds standing to the credit of any policy year or of any reserve account could be pooled and invested either as one fund or as two or more separate funds.

In the event of a catastrophic claim against the association exceeding the limits of the group's market reinsurances, it would in all probability, be necessary for members of the group to make a catastrophe call upon their members to recover the amounts by which such claims have exceeded the reinsurances.

Indeed some of the early hull clubs constructed reserve funds to stand to the credit of each member proportionally so that should contributions not be sufficient for a particular year, such reserves could be used to meet any such deficiency. The early P & I associations did not catch on to this idea until quite late and it was not in fact until the early 1970s that most of the modern clubs realised the potential liabilities, as affected by the very high values of ships and more particularly cargoes. This was combined with the impact of world inflation which was increasing faster than the capacity of the reinsurance market. In order to protect their members from these developments many associations decided to form 'catastrophe' or 'contingency' reserve funds to be used specially for such events. These funds were originally created by a separate element added to the advance call and can now be extended occasionally by underwriting surpluses and the clubs' own investment incomes.

Some P & I associations maintain separate funds, not necessarily for catastrophic claims, but as a hedge against freak years where claims can be unusually high, to protect members from unexpectedly high supplementary calls. These funds, as we have said, are designated in separate accounts such as contingency or reserve funds and by dipping into these reserves a club can usually keep its actual supplementary calls within predicted percentage limits and close its years in accordance with the original estimate of supplementary calls. This has the effect of greatly contributing towards the stability of calls achieved by so many clubs in the face of escalating values and inflation.

RESPONSIBILITY FOR THE PAYMENT OF CALLS

The party responsible for the payment of calls to the club is the member who is contractually bound to the club. Generally it can be said that the owners of the vessel who authorise a person to effect an insurance with and enter as a member of a P & I association are also liable as assureds under the contract for the payment of calls. By the same token such owners must be in a position to bring actions against the club to recover their losses.

In the case of *British Marine Mutual Insurance Company* v. *Jenkins and Others* (1889), the defendant's manager insured the defendant's vessel with the club in his own name and for and in the names of all persons to whom the same right appertained. The articles of association of the club defined the member as any person who, on behalf of himself or of any other person, insured any ship with the club and went on to make the members liable for the payment of calls. The defendants authorised the manager of their ship to enter her in the club and he thereby became a member of the club and was therefore personally liable to pay the calls. When the manager became insolvent and unable to pay the calls, the plaintiff club brought an action against the defendant shipowners as being the persons on whose behalf and for whose benefit the insurance was effected. In his decision Bigham, J decided that the defendants, being the owners of an insurance interest, were the persons for whom the insurance was effected and there was nothing in the club documents to exclude their liability to pay calls. In a situation where there are joint entries, clubs quite commonly provide that the joint members and each of them shall jointly and severally be liable to pay all calls and other sums due to the club in respect of the entry of the particular vessel. In this way the clubs avoid any involvement in the members' partnership rights.

Unless there is an express provision to the contrary it is an implied term of the contract between the club and its members that the right to make calls must be exercised on the basis of equality as between members of the same class.

Where a vessel is not owned by a corporate entity but by co-owners, for example, under the general 'sixty-four parts' scheme, difficulties may arise, for example, where the managing owner put forward by his co-owners as the member of the club fails to pay. Therefore, a part-owner who may be called upon to pay as a defendant of the 'managing-owner member' may not wish to pay all the referred 64 parts and accordingly to prevent this situation arising, which could lead to the withdrawal of the vessel's entry, there is generally a proper management agreement and the entry is effected in the names of the committee of all owners.

Where a member has committed a breach of the club rules so as to have his membership terminated, he does not at the same time relieve himself of his liability to pay out calls which are owed.

RESPONSIBILITY FOR THE COLLECTION OF CALLS

The power to make calls and assess supplementary calls and the discretion as to the frequency and size of those calls usually lie with the committee of the directors of the particular association.

The nature and extent of the directors' discretion in levying supplementary calls was reviewed in the case of *Volkswagenwerk A.G. and Wolfsburger Transport Gesellschaft mbH* v. *International Mutual Strike Assurance Company (Bermuda).* The club involved in the dispute was a strike club which, although insuring against both crew and shore strikes, operated only one common fund for these two forms of risk. One of the issues before the court was a complaint by the plaintiff member of the club regarding the size of the supplementary calls that had been made on him. A member, who was insured only in respect of shore strikes, believed that the reason for the unexpectedly high supplementary calls was a poor claims record on the crew strikes side of the business. The explanation that was given by the club was that there was only one common fund, that the shore strikes had always been considered to be a greater risk than crew strikes and that, although they had considered whether they could increase the supplementary calls on members who were only insured against crew strikes for that particular year, the directors had received legal advice that they could only levy supplementary calls in the same proportion as the advance calls already made. In fact, this legal advice turned out to be incorrect. In accordance with one of the club rules it was open to the directors to levy supplementary calls either at such percentage rate in respect of the contributing value of the ships that were entered or at such percentage of the advance call for such policy year as the directors deemed fit.

The directors had only selected the latter alternative in the mistaken belief that no other choice was open to them and since this was quite clearly wrong, the court decided that the directors had misdirected themselves in the exercise of their discretion and the supplementary calls could not stand.

It was contended by the club that, although calls may have been levied on a basis which is not permissible under its own rules, as the member had paid the calls this payment amounted to waiver of the irregularity. The court, however, rejected this argument as it would have placed the aggrieved members in the position that they would not have to be vigilant as to irregularities and the failure to spot an unlawful call would bar their right to complain.

NON-PAYMENT OF CALLS

To reflect the true spirit of mutuality, any amounts which cannot be collected from members as calls, for example, by virtue of the member's bankruptcy, will have to be made up in some other way, perhaps by the levy of an additional call or by dipping into the reserves. It has been the recent practice of P & I associations to increase the amount initially called up as an advance call and making proportionally smaller supplementary calls. One of the reasons behind this trend is to avoid the danger of default in the payment of supplementary calls. It is normal for club rules to make a provision for such eventualities.

Any member who fails in his duty to pay outstanding calls punctually may be subjected to various sanctions, including the following examples.

Forfeiture of cover

One of the major disincentives against the failure to pay outstanding calls is that the member may be taken off risk and the insurance cover withdrawn, not only from the date of the failure to pay but also in respect of any claims which have arisen prior to the date of non-payment. The power of the clubs in relation to forfeiture for non-payment of premiums was examined in the case of *Williams* v. *The British Mutual Marine Insurance Company* (1887) where the rules of the association provided that if any member should neglect to pay his contributions he should forfeit all claims for any loss. The club in that particular case claimed a contribution from the plaintiff member who responded by claiming to set off a sum due to him on the same vessel in the previous year in respect of losses which were owed to him by the club. The club eventually refused to allow the set-off and declared the claim as forfeited. A loss occurred and a claim was made and refused by the club. The court was accordingly asked whether the club had the right to forfeit under these circumstances. It was decided that the set-off was a mutual settlement which was equivalent to payment of the calls and there could not, therefore, be any forfeiture.

Payment of interest

Some of the old hull clubs imposed fines on those members who failed to pay calls punctually. Although the modern P & I associations have not persisted with this practice, club rules do generally provide the committee of directors with the power to charge interest on calls which are due to them and have not been paid by the date specified. These rules provide the committee with an absolute discretion as to the rate of interest payable and such rates of interest can be as much as 20% per annum.

Inability to obtain new cover

A member of a club who is in arrears with his club calls can incur difficulties in obtaining cover from another P & I club.

Although there is no express agreement between the clubs on this matter, when a member applies for membership of a new club he will invariably be asked to provide details of his claims record and calls record from his previous club. Where the previous records show a poor performance in respect of the payment of calls it is unlikely that the new club would accept the application.

Proceeding against the entered vessel

NO LIENS

In quite a number of jurisdictions, including the United States, mutual insurance contracts in relation to property insurance provide for the granting of liens on the insured property of the assured for assessments and contributions. In some jurisdictions insurers have a maritime lien in respect of unpaid premiums or at least the right to arrest the vessel of an assured who owes outstanding premiums to his insurer.

*

In the United Kingdom P & I associations in common with other insurers, are unable to proceed against the vessel for recovery of calls. No action *in rem* exists in respect of marine insurance premiums under the Supreme Court Act 1981.

The Brussels Arrest Convention of 1952 (International Convention Relating to the Arrest of Seagoing Ships, signed at Brussels, 10 May 1952) does not include claims for insurance premiums among the list of claims for which an action *in rem* is available. As a consequence of this insurers have attempted to proceed against the entered vessel in respect of unpaid premiums under other heads of *in rem* action.

The case of *West of England Shipowners Mutual P & I Association (Luxembourg)* v. *Aifanourios Shipping SA (The 'Aifanourios')* decided that an agreement for marine insurance cover was not an 'agreement relating to the use or hire of any ship', nor was it a 'necessary' so as to grant a right of action *in rem* within the relevant Scottish provisions which are broadly equivalent to what was section 1(1)(*h*) of the Administration of Justice Act 1956 and what is now section 29(2)(*h*) of the Supreme Court Act 1981. The case itself concerned an agreement between shipowners and P & I clubs for the entry of a vessel in the club. On the failure of the shipowner to pay release calls the club arrested the vessel and moved for its sale to satisfy the debt owed to the club in respect of unpaid calls. The defendant shipowner challenged the competence of the court to deal with the action as an action *in rem*. The catalogue of claims which entitled a claimant to proceed with an action *in rem* in the courts of Scotland are stated in section 42(2) of the Administration of Justice Act 1956 which provided: 'This section applies to any claim arising and to one or more of the following, that is to say . . . (d) any agreement relating to the use or hire of any ship whether by charter or otherwise'.

The judge held that an insurance agreement was not an agreement connected with the use of the ship, it was more a matter directed to the convenience or protection of the owner.

In the recent case of *The 'Sandrina', Gatoil International Inc.* v. *Arkwright Boston Manufacturers Mutual Insurance Company and Others*, the House of Lords was required to consider a claim by cargo underwriters to arrest a vessel allegedly owned by various assureds in respect of unpaid premiums on a cargo. The assured vessel had been arrested in Scotland under section 47(2)(e) of the Administration of Justice Act 1956 which provided the right to arrest the vessel in respect of a claim arising out of the following: '(e) in the agreement relating to the carriage of goods in a ship by charter-party or otherwise'.

The House of Lords decided that for an agreement to come within the terms of this provision it must not only be one 'relating to the carriage of goods in a ship' but also the relationship between that agreement and the carriage of goods in a ship must be direct or very close and not merely in some way connected, however remotely, to the carriage of goods in a ship or with the use or hire of a ship. The court accordingly held in that case the contract of marine insurance was not connected with the carriage of goods in a ship in a sufficiently direct sense to be capable of coming within the appropriate section of the Administration of Justice Act 1956.

The current position, therefore, is that claims arising out of contracts of marine insurance are not claims which entitle a claimant to proceed by way of action *in rem* and clubs claiming in respect of P & I club membership are in no better position than those claiming in respect of traditional hull and cargo insurance.

SET-OFF

Normally club rules state that no claim by a member against the club shall constitute any set-off against the calls or other sums owing to the club. Such a situation would not entitle a member to withhold or delay any payment due to the club. In spite of these provisions a set-off may be made at the discretion of the particular club. A club rule dealing with set-offs and counterclaims may state as follows:

> 'Without prejudice to anything elsewhere contained in these rules it shall be a condition precedent of a member's right to recover from the funds of the association in respect of any liabilities, costs or expenses that all such calls and other amounts whatsoever that shall have become due from the member to the association shall have been paid in full by the member or by some assignee or other person on his behalf provided that: the committee shall have power in its sole discretion to waive the above condition, but in such event the association shall be entitled to set off any amounts due from a member against any amount due to him from the association.'

There are numerous examples of how such situations may occur. For example, a member may have two or more vessels entered in the same club and have a claim relating to one of his entered vessels but owe money to the club in respect of the other. In such a case the rule may entitle the club to a right of set-off against the member. However, should the shipowner have taken the step of establishing 'one-ship' companies to own his vessels so that each vessel is entered by its owning company then, preserving the principle of the separate entity of each owner, the club would not be in a position to set off an amount owing from one separate member against amounts owing to another member.

RETURN OF CALLS

Under the Marine Insurance Act 1906 (section 84), in a traditional marine insurance contract, if the risk has never commenced then the premium will be returned. In the case of mutual insurance, however, there is an exception to this general principle which can arise because of the dual capacity of the club member. The member of a P & I association has rights not only as an assured but also has duties as an insurer or contributor to the losses of his fellow members. A member will continue to be liable for the payment of calls even after his insurance protection has been withdrawn because of his failure to abide by the club rules. The reason for this is that membership is something which exists independently of the actual right of a particular member to be insured. The calls payable by a member are therefore an indication of two roles and represent not only premium but also his share of the insurance settlement.

Some associations do make provision for the return of premiums where membership ceases at an unexpectedly early time and there are club rules which provide that where entry is terminated at other than the expiration of the insurance year or other period originally agreed, the club may make a pro rata return of the advance calls. Some clubs also make specific provisions for return of the advance calls in the case of the total loss of the entered vessel.

Laid-up returns

On the basis that whilst a vessel is laid up the risks attaching to the vessel are diminished, club rules generally provide for adjustments to be made by way of returns to the member during periods when the entered vessel is laid up or is being repaired.

Clubs may provide that the advance call may be returned only where the period of lay-up or repairs is for a specified period, usually of 30 consecutive days, and this provision is on the basis that there is no cargo on board during the period of lay-up. Clubs will also ensure that in those instances where a premium is returned due to lay-up, sufficient premium is retained to cover reinsurance and administrative costs for the laid-up vessel and to provide port risks cover.

There are generally provisions for two classes of lay-up, first the short period of lay-up where a vessel is laid-up with full crew and/or cargo and secondly, the more prolonged lay-up where the vessel has no cargo on board and no crew. In both these cases the vessel must be in a 'safe port'.

In the first instance members are normally entitled to up to 50% return of premiums, whereas in the second the return can be as much as 95% when the vessel is laid up for 30 days or more. Club rules will generally provide that no claim for laid-up returns shall be recoverable from the club unless written notice thereof has been given to the club within a particular specified period, often a period of six months after the end of the policy year concerned. Members will also be required to notify the club as soon as a laid-up vessel recommences her trading. This is in order to enable the club, should it decide to do so, to survey the vessel. Should a member fail to notify the club of the recommencement of trading or fail to give an opportunity of having his vessel surveyed, the club can avoid liability for any losses which could have been avoided if the opportunity for such survey had been given or a survey had been carried out and any defects revealed in that survey had been remedied.

Another limit imposed on a member's entitlement to recover returns in respect of periods of lay-up is as from the time that the vessel shall have been agreed by hull underwriters as constituting a constructive total loss or a compromised total loss.

Whilst the vessel is not navigating, although continuing to be entered with the P & I associations for that cover, owners have sometimes been tempted to cancel their hull insurances. From the point of view of his P & I cover this could prove to be an inadvisable step for a member to take. According to club rules a member is presumed to have the usual and customary hull insurance cover up to the vessel's full value and this requirement will persist even in time of lay-up. Owners should, therefore, either continue their hull cover or effect the most extensive hull port risks insurance cover. Failure to do this may severely prejudice a member's P & I club protection under the rule which deems him to have full hull cover because this rule would appear to apply to the vessel whether or not it is navigating.

RELEASE CALLS

In circumstances where a member's entry with his club is terminated, the club, without waiting to call for contributions for the financial year, will usually determine an individual additional premium based on the anticipated rate of contribution for the year. The payment of this call allows the retiring member to be 'released' from his obligations for future calls in respect of his period of entry. As such, this payment is appropriately known as a release call.

In the absence of such a mechanism a club would have the burden of pursuing their ex-members for periods of up to possibly five or more years after the time that they have left the club for contributions owing in respect of their period of insurance. Not only do release calls relieve the clubs of this burden but also enable the ex-member to be free of future liabilities in respect of his particular period of insurance. It may be that on leaving the club the member gives up the business of shipowning entirely and it would be an intolerable situation for both club and the ex-member in such circumstances to be involved in negotiation for sums due in respect of policy years which have elapsed many years previously.

A MEMBER'S DUTY TO ACT AS PRUDENT UNINSURED

If a member of a P & I association incurs a casualty to one of his vessels which gives rise to a claim on the association, a member cannot merely notify the club, sit back and do nothing. The member in such circumstances is under a duty, on behalf of the association, himself and legally, to take steps to minimise any loss and to prevent further loss; in other words he must conduct himself as if he were not entered in the association and indeed had no insurance. This duty involves the member in taking steps to exclude or mitigate his loss. A failure by the member to conduct himself in this manner empowers the club, at the discretion of the committee or board of directors, to deduct a sum from that member's claim in an amount within the discretion of the committee.

This particular rule is consistent with the general principles of marine insurance law as expressed in the Marine Insurance Act 1906 which provides in section 78(4) as follows: '. . . it is the duty of the assured and his agents, in all cases to take such measures as may be reasonable for the purpose of averting or minimising a loss.'

In order to make it clear that the member is under a duty to sue and labour and to act as an uninsured shipowner, these duties are expressly stated in P & I club rules to ensure 'that upon the occurrence of any casualty, event or other matter liable to give rise to a claim, by a member upon the association, it should be the duty of that member and/or his agents to take and continue to take all such steps as may be reasonable for the purpose of averting or minimising any expense or liability in respect whereof he may be insured by the association'.

If a member commits any breach of this obligation to sue and labour and to act as a prudent uninsured the committee of the association may at its discretion reject any claims by the member against the association arising out of the casualty under consideration.

This rule imposed the duty on the member to minimise loss and to act as an uninsured shipowner at the time of the 'occurrence of any casualty, event or matter liable to give rise to a claim.' The fact that the duty is said to arise on the occurrence of any casualty or claim liable to give rise to a claim against the club is a feature necessitated by the peculiar nature of P & I insurance coverage. In the case of *Xenos* v. *Fox* (1868), it was held that the sue and labour clause did not introduce a new subject matter of insurance into the policy. In this case Cockburn, CJ, concluded his opinion on the operation of the clause with the statement: 'If damages had been recovered by the owners of the "*Mars*" against the plaintiff that would have brought the case within the clause.' From this it appears that the sue and labour clause does not come into operation until a loss covered by the policy has occurred.

An essential feature of indemnity insurance provided by the P & I Associations is that no loss within club cover is deemed to have occurred until a member has been adjudicated liable and has discharged that liability.

The sue and labour clause, if worded as in the previously mentioned case of *Xenos* v. *Fox*, would be rendered null and void by virtue of the fact that it would not be brought into operation until judgment was entered against the member and his payment of that judgment debt. It is for this reason that it has been held that P & I club insurers are not responsible, under sue and labour provisions, for the legal costs of successfully defending a claim.

The consequences of a breach of the duty imposed by the Marine Insurance Act 1906 are uncertain and in the case of P & I club rules, although more certain, there would appear to be some divergence amongst the rules of the various clubs as to the sanctions to be applied upon members who fail in the duty imposed by the rules.

Some club rules give discretion to the committee to reject the claim, or the extent to which a claim may be reduced are based upon the connection between the breach of the obligation and the occurrence or size of the eventual claim. Some club rules make the observance of the rule a condition precedent to a member's right of recovery, albeit with the discretion vested in the committee, to admit claims where there has been a breach.

Having imposed the duty to take measures to reduce or minimise claims, club rules go on to provide, with certain qualifications, for the reimbursement of the expenses incurred by the member in complying with his duty. The expenses which clubs are prepared to cover are 'extraordinary costs and expenses'. Generally this phrase is not defined in club rule books nor is it used in the sue and labour provisions of the Marine Insurance Act 1906. The phrase is, however, compatible with the words used in the definition of general average in section 66 of the Marine Insurance Act 1906 and assistance in construing this phrase may be gained from this branch of maritime law. In the law of general average, extraordinary expenditure is something more than those ordinary disbursements which are necessary for keeping the ship in a proper condition to carry out its trade. Some clubs have gone some way in attempting to define the phrase stating that it covers the cost of measures which 'are reasonably incurred to fulfil the owner's obligation to sue and labour to avert and minimise any loss, damage, liability, cost or expense. The club, however, has a discretion to reject or make a deduction from claims where the owner has failed to fulfil his obligation.'

DISPUTES BETWEEN A MEMBER AND HIS CLUB

The legality of using clauses which seek to force members of an association to submit to arbitration as a condition precedent to going to the courts of law was tested in the case of *Scott* v. *Avery* (1876). The case itself, which gave rise to the well-known 'Scott and Avery clause', concerned an arbitration clause in the rules of the Newcastle A1 Insurance Association which was a mutual marine hull association.

The decision of the House of Lords in this case was that it is a principle of law that parties cannot by contract oust the jurisdiction of the courts, but any party may covenant that no right of action shall accrue until a third party has decided on any difference that may arise between the two parties to the contract.

P & I associations invariably include a rule which, in the case of disputes between the club and member, makes submission to arbitration a condition precedent to the right of a member to bring an action. The contents of such a rule stipulate that if there is any difference or dispute arising between a member and the association out of or in connection with the rules of that association or as to the rights or obligations of the association, such difference or dispute should be referred to arbitration. It should be normal for London arbitration to be nominated and that a sole legal arbitrator be appointed. Again it is normal for such an arbitrator to be a practising Queen's Counsel of the commercial bar or indeed any other practising Queen's Counsel and the submission to arbitration and all the proceedings shall be subject to the provisions of the Arbitration Acts.

Some clubs state that if there is any difference or dispute between the member and the club, then such dispute may in the first instance be referred to and adjudicated by the directors of the association on written submissions. Only where the member does not accept the decision of the directors shall the dispute be referred to arbitration. The reason for such a referral is that the club will not resort to outside assistance until the member's own fellow members, the directors, have exhausted all possibilities of an amicable and inexpensive settlement.

Where there is a rule which requires disputes to be referred to the committee it is necessary that the proceedings of the committee in investigating and adjudicating upon the matter should be conducted in a regular and impartial manner.

4
SCOPE OF P & I CLUB COVER

As explained in chapter 1, the risks covered by a P & I club's rules were not drafted out in 'one fell swoop' by some insurance broker by candlelight on a three-legged stool with a quill pen, but evolved over a number of years with new risks being added as and when a major law suit or significant statutory innovation created the need. To say that the clubs cover everything not covered by some other policy of insurance would not be too wide of the mark, and to say that the clubs were a receptacle for all risks unplaceable elsewhere sounds disparaging, but nevertheless reasonably describes the position. A true enough brief description of a P & I insurer is that he covers shipowners (or whomever) against their legal liabilities to third parties. One essential element, benefiting members and club managers alike, is the flexibility of the rules. This is illustrated in what is known as the omnibus rule, a 'catch all' provision inserted at the end of the list of specific risks covered and which is designed to allow a member to submit a claim for recovery from the association which does not fall squarely under the head of any specific rule. The omnibus rule, which will be commented upon later, is discretionary, meaning that a claim in connection with the business of shipowning will be given consideration by the committee of the association who will accept it or reject it as they think fit.

Although the clubs started as protection clubs only and became indemnity clubs later, the difference between protection risks and indemnity risks has no practical significance, except perhaps that the protection risks tend to be connected with ownership and the indemnity risks connected with the employment of the ship.

LEGALITY OF INDEMNITY INSURANCE

When the concept of insurance was in its infancy many doubts were raised as to its efficacy in that the financial protection afforded to the assured, it was argued, removed the need to take care in relation to the object of insurance. In 1741 the Admiralty recorded a minute on the number of vessels in wartime convoy that insisted on breaking away and racing ahead to get their cargo to the market before those who were both their companions and competitors. This mischief had developed, it was believed, because of the recent practice of insurance. Ships' masters, safe in the knowledge that both vessel and cargo were fully insured, took the calculated risk of breaking convoy in order to obtain better prices.

Although the mechanism of insurance has now attained acceptance and respectability it is not surprising that the development of liability and indemnity insurance, designed to compensate assureds in respect of the consequences of their wrongdoing, should be viewed with suspicion. Many are of the view that indemnity insurance removes the financial deterrent against an assured's wrongdoing.

Although P & I clubs cover shipowners for numerous types of costs and expenses which arise totally without fault, for example, expenses of stowaways, quarantine expenses, repatriation costs and others, the major part of club cover is designed to indemnify members in respect of liabilities they have incurred by virtue of their fault or the fault of their servants. As a member is, therefore, generally seeking an indemnity in respect of a liability which he has incurred and discharged arising from his fault, questions of legality are likely to arise.

In the first half of the 19th century it was generally considered to be contrary to public policy to allow a person to insure against the consequences of his own negligence or that of his servants. In *Delanoy* v. *Robson* it was said: 'It would be an illegal insurance to insure against what might be the consequences of the wrongful acts of the assured.'

The principle was explained in *Burrows* v. *Rhodes* by Kennedy, J in the following terms:

'It has, I think, long been settled law that if an act is manifestly unlawful, or the doer of it knows it to be unlawful . . . he cannot maintain an action for contribution or for indemnity against the liability which results therefrom. An express provision of indemnity to him for the commission of such act is void.'

Even where the carelessness was on the part of the assured's servants Benecket, writing in 1824, stated:

'The damages occasioned to a ship and her cargo by being run foul of accidentally, and without fault on either side, ought to be particular average and is so by the civil law, as well as by the law of England (*Buller* v. *Fisher*, 1800), which considers such an injury as a peril of the sea. . . . The underwriters are liable, unless it be proved that the loss was attributable to the negligence of the master or crew of the ship insured.'

Even by the end of the 19th century doubts were still being expressed as to the efficacy of marine insurance. In an article by Captain A G Fround, secretary of the Shipmasters' Society of London, it is argued:

'A good deal of the recklessness and apathy shown by shipowners and speculators is to be accounted for by the possibility of insuring in full against loss of ship, cargo, and even unsecured freight. Indeed, unlimited insurance has unquestionably done much toward cheapening life upon the ocean.'

The general view was that negligent conduct should be punished and not compensated for or rewarded. This view persisted to an extent even until the introduction of the running down clause, which is thought to be the first attempt to insure against liabilities. At the time of its introduction many insurers were opposed to it and in 1850 and 1854 underwriters from Lloyd's petitioned the Board of Trade to have the use of the clause outlawed. Such petitions, of course, failed but the demand that the assured should bear one-fourth of collision liabilities under the running down clause was an attempt to ensure that the shipowner continued to have some interest to protect and some concern for the preservation of his interest.

A good deal of learned attention has been devoted to the legality and morality of liability insurance but it suffices to say that attitudes have changed in relation to liability insurance in general and to marine insurance in particular. It is probably fair to say that the notion of outlawing liability insurance as being a provoker of illegal and inconceivable acts is now

IMMORAL?

NEGLECT SHOULD BE PUNISHED NOT COMPENSATED FOR?!

something of a dated view. Indeed, there have even been calls from some quarters in support of establishing a system of compulsory marine liability insurance.

The type of cover provided by P & I clubs is now recognised as entirely legitimate. Section 506 of the Merchant Shipping Act 1894 recognises the validity of insurance for shipowners in respect of their liability to pay damages for loss of life, injury or damage in the circumstances listed in section 503 of the Act. Further, the Marine Insurance Act 1906 also recognises the right of a shipowner to insure against his liabilities to third parties. Section 3(1) provides that every lawful marine adventure may be the subject of a contract of marine insurance and sub-section (2) provides that there is a marine adventure where, *inter alia*, '(c) Any liability to a third party may be incurred by the owner of, or any other person interested in or responsible for, insurable property, by reason of maritime perils'. This provision goes on to define maritime perils as follows:

'"Maritime perils" means the perils consequent on, or incidental to, the navigation of the sea, that is to say, perils of the seas, fire, war perils, pirates, rovers, thieves, captures, seizures, restraints, and detainments of princes and peoples, jettisons, barratry, and any other perils either of the like kind, or which may be designated by the policy.'

The phrase 'any other perils, either of the like kind, or which may be designated by the policy', would also cover liability insurance in that the word 'peril' can be interpreted as meaning 'risk' in the sense of the risk of incurring a liability to another person in connection with a specific object or under a certain obligation.

Marine liability insurance is recognised later in the 1906 Act when dealing with the measure of indemnity, where section 74 provides: 'Where the assured has effected an insurance in express terms against any liability to a third party, the measure of indemnity, subject to any express provision in the policy, is the amount paid or payable by him to such third party in respect of such liability.'

In the recent case of *The 'Agathon'*, Hobhouse, J recognised the legitimacy of hull underwriters covering liabilities in respect of running down and for general average contributions and salvage as well as other liabilities and decided that a shipowner's interest in his vessel includes the avoidance of exposure to liability. As regards a shipowner's liability for cargo carried on board his vessel, it was settled quite early that he could insure against his liabilities as a carrier.

Before commencing commentary on each specified risk covered under P & I rules, it is as well to emphasise that by the very nature of P & I cover members can only obtain benefit of the cover provided under the P & I class where loss, damage, liability or expense which he has incurred arises in respect of his interest in an entered ship, secondly where such loss, etc. arises out of events which occurred during the period of entry of that particular entered ship in the association and thirdly where such loss, etc. arises in connection with the operation of the particular ship. These may seem obvious preconditions to the right of recovery, but nevertheless it is not uncommon for members of clubs to expect recovery where one or more of these conditions has not been complied with.

RISKS INSURED AGAINST UNDER CLUB COVER

Loss of life, personal injury, illness

Clubs differentiate between crewmen and others. Crew members are indemnified in respect of compensation or damages for which shipowners have a liability to pay as a result of injury, illness or death of a seaman during his period of service on board or during the periods of proceeding to or from the entered vessel. Also recoverable from funds are hospital, medical and funeral expenses. It is provided that any costs or expenses incurred because of the terms/contract of employment and arising directly from them and which would not otherwise have been incurred would only be recoverable if the terms of employment had received the prior approval of the club managers.

In the United States the Jones Act which was introduced in 1921 is a Federal Act which gave a cause of action to crewmen, originally on American vessels, to sue their employers for injuries suffered in the course of their employment. The basis of liability under the Jones Act was and still is the establishing of negligence against the employer and the slightest degree of negligence is sufficient to persuade an American court that liability exists for which damages should be awarded. A further entitlement of a seaman under the Jones Act is a trial by jury and it is well known that jury awards in the United States are generous in the extreme since it is they, not the presiding judge, who has the right to pronounce not only on liability on the evidence before them but also to assess the damages if liability is found. The protection of the Jones Act is now extended to foreign seamen on the basis of their showing that there is a substantial contact with the United States in the facts and circumstances of the incident which gives rise to the loss or injury which in turn provides them with the cause of action.

Death or injury of stevedores is dealt with by a separate rule which defines that category of persons as those persons 'engaged to handle the cargo of the entered vessel'. The ability to recover is qualified by a proviso saying that the liabilities, costs, expenses in respect of which recovery is sought should arise from an act, neglect or default on board or in relation to the insured vessel or in relation to the cargo handling. The area where the clubs as a group find themselves exposed to claims on a massive aggregate scale is the USA where the practice of bringing claims on a common law basis through the courts against shipowners or indeed anyone with an interest in the vessel (e.g. particularly a time charterer) based on negligence (which the plaintiff must prove) is particularly rife. It would be true to say that the two types of claim which in aggregate have proved year by year the most expensive for the clubs are personal injury and cargo (with cargo perhaps 'topping the bill' now but only because of the high and still rising values of many cargoes). It is US jurisdiction which has ensured these high statistics in personal injury/death. To some extent these high awards via the courts for these types of claim may be attributed to the jury system, it being the jury, as already mentioned, which pronounces on liability after direction by the judge on the law and also assesses damages.

An illustration of a serious value personal injury case was a case which was litigated on the west coast of the United States (District of California) in recent times. The facts were that a third officer of an American flag vessel decided for reasons best known to himself that he was being persecuted on board by the rest of the crew, and took one of the ship's life-rafts in the very early hours of one morning when the ship was 1,000 miles east of the Bahamas. He lowered himself on the raft over the stern of the ship and disappeared into the night. A member of the crew on watch said later, that he 'thought he heard a splash' but thought no more about it. The following morning when the officer was discovered missing the master turned the ship about and retraced his tracks but was unable to discover the man and so continued on his way. The man was picked up about two days later by a passing vessel and brought to Cardiff in the UK where he was examined by a doctor and found to be in reasonably good physical and psychological shape. He was repatriated unescorted back to his home state of California where soon afterwards he brought an action against the owners of his vessel for damages for nervous shock and/or mental anguish caused by his alleged treatment whilst on board the ship. The managers of the owner's club engaged Californian lawyers to investigate the matter and various crew members were interviewed, including the master, who said that he was aware that the man was of a nervous disposition and took care not to keep him on elongated watches and provided him with tranquillisers from the ship's medical box. The remainder of the crew were told to treat him with 'reasonably kid gloves' and efforts were made within the confines of the ship to make his life as bearable as possible. The man's own lawyer claimed that his client was unable to get a job or even to work again and that the 'nightmare' two-day period on the life-raft not knowing whether he would be picked up or not and drifting out of the sea lanes, had caused irreparable damage to his mental state. His only chance of work was as an attendant at his uncle's 'merry-go-round'. He was a 'lad' in his mid-twenties with all his life before him.

Despite these 'sorrowful' facts the committee of the owner's P & I club, to whom this case had been reported, were quite unwilling to meet the US$700,000 demand to settle this claim and resolved to prepare a defence for presentation in the California District Court. This was done and the man was examined by a psychiatrist on behalf of the owners of the vessel. The matter went through a seven-day trial, during which medical evidence was predominant and two opposing psychiatrists maintained fundamentally different views of when, where and how the man had originated what appeared to be his 'persecution mania'. His own psychiatrist claimed that prior to his service on board he was a normal human being with a perfectly usual behaviour pattern and that it was totally the treatment by the master and the fellow crew members which had caused him to become in the state which he now found himself in. The owners' psychiatrist said that his nervous disposition had long pre-existed his service on board and could be traced back to his childhood. At the end of seven days the jury brought in an award in favour of the seaman of US$1,650,000 which even in the early 1980s was a considerable amount of money.

Other benefits which a member can obtain from his club are, in relation to his crew, compensation which he may have been obliged to pay for the loss of employment resulting from the loss or wreck of a vessel (known as shipwreck unemployment indemnity), wages of a crewman during hospitalisation or treatment abroad or while awaiting or during repatriation, and reimbursement of expenses incurred in sending substitute crew abroad or repatriating a substitute necessarily engaged abroad. Repatriation expenses are also recoverable if the reason for the repatriation is not that the man himself is ill or needs home treatment but he is essentially required to attend a wife, child or in the case of a single man a parent who has fallen ill.

Seamen's effects

The clubs will reimburse a member who has incurred a liability to make good a claim for loss or damage to personal effects of crew, but effects in this context do not include cash, negotiable instruments or stones or objects of a rare or valuable nature unless there has been prior agreement between member and managers. Where the liability to compensation has arisen under contract then club coverage is conditional upon the terms of that contract having had the manager's prior written approval.

Passengers

Clubs cover the member's risk of liability in respect of death, injury or illness to passengers travelling under some sort of contract of passage, a condition precedent to such cover is that the club should have approved beforehand the terms and conditions of the contract of passage. One of the clauses which in earlier times enabled a carrier of passengers to avoid liability was the exclusion clause exempting a carrier from the negligence of himself or his servants or agents, which caused death or injury to a passenger. This clause, to be found as a routine in all passenger tickets, judicially lost favour with the English courts and finally received a statutory 'outlawing' in 1978 with the introduction of the Unfair Contract Terms Act (section 2). Thus the test of negligence is now the main basis for the bringing of a suit against an owner for damages for death or injury of a passenger.

Equally importantly, the clubs are concerned in the calculation of limitation available to a carrier of passengers. Hereto, trends have developed apace this decade by the coming into international effect of both the Athens (1974) and the London (1976) Conventions. The former is a specialist convention on the carriage of passengers and their baggage by sea and the latter is a convention on maritime claims generally.

Strangely, if not irritatingly, the two conventions have seemingly conflicting provisions for limitation. The UK has ratified both conventions and both have been absorbed into English law. The Athens Convention allows a shipowner to limit to 46,666 units of account for *each* passenger injured (subject to an absence of any reckless conduct by the carrier himself, or his alter ego, which might have contributed to the accident), whereas the London Convention provides for a limitation fund to be calculated by multiplying the number of passengers which the ship is capable (by licence) of carrying by 46,666 units. The Athens Convention talks about 'each carriage', i.e. each voyage, the London Convention about 'each distinct occasion'.

The Athens Convention became law before the London

Convention, the latter becoming law on 1 December 1986. Since then no disaster involving passengers has tested the point in court. The tragedy of the *Herald of Free Enterprise* was resolved by out of court payments of compensation exceeding the limitation figures and thus discussion never took place as to whether limitation should or should not be denied. The inter-convention conflict therefore still awaits judicial resolution.

Charterers very rarely become involved in passenger liability though it can be imagined that they might have exposure particularly if, where they are obliged to do so by charter-party terms, they supply certain crew members and become vicariously liable for the consequences of the acts, neglects or defaults of that crew, e.g. stewards or catering staff. One cause of action available to passengers relates to food poisoning and as this illness frequently strikes an entire shipload of passengers, a 'class' action may be brought against the owner by one passenger suing in the name of all.

Wives and children

In the post World War II period it became a practice for many owning companies to allow their masters and officers (and in some cases crewmen) to have their wives and/or children accompany them, especially on long haul voyages. In the early days of this marine 'social' development, owners insisted on the dependent wife signing hold harmless agreements or taking out some form of personal accident cover on her own behalf and on behalf of the children. As this practice grew and became almost a 'custom of the trade' clubs dropped this requirement and offered their owner members' families cover as wide as they gave for the officers or crewmen themselves, i.e. hospital, medical, funeral expenses and repatriation expenses, the last of these not only in respect of the wife's own need to be repatriated but also if it is her husband who requires repatriation. The cover will also include the wife's need to accompany a child who may require to be repatriated if he or she becomes dangerously ill during the voyage.

Diversion expenses

Deviation (the geographical diverting of a ship deliberately from its contractual routing for some particular purpose) is always justified under the general maritime law when the sole and only purpose is to save, or attempt to save, life or for some similar humanitarian reason, whether the life to be saved is on board the diverted vessel or on another vessel to which the diverted vessel may be moving in answer to a distress call. On this legal basis, it is natural to find a rule within ordinary club cover which allows recovery by an owner or member for those *net* expenses incurred in the nature of bunkers, insurance, wages, stores, provisions and port charges, net meaning over and above such of those expenses which would have been incurred but for the diversion.

The only other proviso for recovery of these expenses is that they should have been reasonably incurred and for no other reason than that stated in the relevant rule as described above.

Fines

The scope of cover under this heading embraces fines imposed by a court, tribunal or authority and the following specific list is included:

(1) Breach of a statute or regulation relating to the provision of a safe system of work or working conditions.
(2) Short or over delivery of cargo or failure to comply with the regulations as to declaration of goods or documentation as to cargo.
(3) Smuggling or infringement of any customs regulation.
(4) Breach of immigration regulations.
(5) Incidents in respect of the discharge or escape of oil or other hazardous substances from the entered ship.
(6) Any act or neglect of the seamen of the entered ship or any other servant or agent of the member.

It is provided in this rule that the fine which is the subject of a recovery from the club must have been imposed upon the *member* and if it was imposed upon an agent or seaman then it must be one for which the member is liable or at least liable to reimburse that person. Another proviso is that a fine resulting from the wilful misconduct of a seaman will only be reimbursed if either the member has been compelled by law to pay such fine or had reasonably paid the fine in order to obtain the release from arrest of the entered vessel or any other vessel which he owns.

Oil pollution

This head of cover is chronologically one of the latest risks to be added to the widening spread of P & I cover. The cover given is in respect of the liabilities, losses, damages, costs and expenses in so far as they are caused by or incurred by reason of the discharge or escape of oil or any hazardous substance from the entered vessel, or due to the threat of such discharge or escape. This includes TOVALOP (Tanker Owners' Voluntary Agreement concerning Liability for Oil Pollution) liabilities. It also includes the costs of measures taken to avoid or minimise pollution or of any measures to prevent an imminent danger of the discharge or escape from the entered vessel of oil or any hazardous substance.

Though this book is not intended to be a law text it is a fact that an understanding of the extent of a club's cover for oil pollution would be improved by a brief explanation of the development of tanker owners' liabilities over the past 20 years. 1969 was the year of the *Torrey Canyon* disaster off the UK coast. It was the first of the major pollution incidents of recent times and the world was caught entirely unawares and unequipped to know how and from what source to compensate innocent victims. The UK had nothing but the common law to turn to for a regime of liability and damages. However, in the aftermath of the *Torrey Canyon*, it was not international legislation which came first but rather a voluntary agreement between tanker owners (known as TOVALOP) to contribute money for the purpose of compensating governments who were obliged to bear the cost of cleaning up their coastlines. One object of this voluntary scheme was to relieve innocent victims of the burden of having to find some regime of liability which would give them a basis for claiming and a sympathetic court which would give ear to their complaint.

Eventually, 98% of the world's ocean going tanker fleet took part in the scheme and bareboat charterers could join the scheme as well as registered owners. It has other features which differ from the Convention on Civil Liability (CLC) which followed in the same year, 1969. First, TOVALOP is applicable to acts concerned in removing a mere threat of an escape of oil, secondly, a spill from a tanker in *ballast* comes within the scheme and, thirdly, the tanker owner's right to limit his liability cannot be denied him (as it can under CLC), the limit being $160 per tonne or US$16.8 million maximum.

Funds available from the TOVALOP supplement of 1987 are calculated on the basis of a minimum grt of 5,000 for which US$3.5 million are available. To this are added US$493 per grt for each tonne over 5,000 up to 140,000 grt. Over 140,000 the compensation is fixed at US$70,000,000. The supplementary TOVALOP, effective from 20 February 1987, only applies in circumstances where the CRISTAL (Contract Regarding an Interim Supplement to Tanker Liability for Oil Pollution) Agreement is applicable. CRISTAL is, like TOVALOP, a creature of industry, although of the oil industry itself and not the tanker industry which gave birth to TOVALOP. Thus, because the contributors to CRISTAL are oil men and not tanker men, the P & I clubs have no concern in the funds paid out by CRISTAL. CRISTAL, as it stands at present, will provide supplementary compensation on the following scale:

Up to 5,000 grt—US$36,000,000

Over 5,000 and up to 140,000 grt—US$36,000,000 plus US$733 per grt

140,000 grt and over—US$135,000,000

A condition precedent to the provision of these funds is that the ship is carrying a CRISTAL cargo at the time.

TOVALOP was never intended to be more than a temporary stop-gap scheme to bridge the gap until a competent international regime of liability and limitation was brought into being. It is a measure of the reluctance of sovereign powers to take upon themselves schemes of liability which bind their citizens that TOVALOP (which was initially forecast to have a life of about three years) should still be in existence in the late 1980s.

The Civil Liability Convention (CLC), drafted in 1969 but

not destined to achieve international effect until 1975, imposed a regime of strict liability on tankers which polluted the territory of a contracting state, but at the same time allowed the offending tanker's registered owner to limit his liability in the absence of personal fault or privity. Under CLC provisions oil must be actually *spilt* for the convention to apply. It applies only to tankers laden with a cargo of persistent crude and not to tankers in ballast or dry cargo vessels. Limitation is 133 SDRs per limitation tonne or 14 million SDRs whichever is the lesser. The Jamaica Protocol of 1984 considerably raises the limits to 3 million SDRs (minimum) for a ship up to 5,000 grt with an additional 420 SDRs for each additional tonne up to an overall maximum of 59.7 million SDRs which is reached at 140,000 grt. Limitation under the protocol will be broken by *reckless conduct*. The 1984 (Jamaica) Protocol is not yet in force and it may be some years yet before it is.

Other major amendments which will come about under its provisions include the following. First, the abolition of the concept (informally called 'roll-back relief') involving an arrangement parallel to the fund convention provision whereby the fund paid back to the offending tanker owner 25% of his liability. Secondly, ballasted tankers will come within the CLC's scope, thus bringing CLC in line with TOVALOP. Thirdly, parties exempted from exposure to CLC claims will be the owners' servants/agents and time charterers or salvors. Fourthly, 'pure threat' situations will be covered so that no oil need be actually spilt (again this will be in line with TOVALOP).

So it is that the clubs have committed themselves to covering the 'patchwork quilt' of liabilities, losses, damages, costs and expenses to which a tanker owner is exposed either as a participant in TOVALOP or as a potential defendant under a CLC-based legal action; this will, of course, mean costs and expenses incurred to avoid a threat even before an actual discharge had occurred (TOVALOP).

Clubs provide for their members evidence of financial capability to comply with their obligations under CLC to prove that they can meet their CLC liability maximum.

Under article 7 of the CLC the owner of a tanker carrying more than 2,000 tonnes of persistent oil in bulk as *cargo* is required to maintain insurance or some other financial security of a capacity sufficient to meet the limits of liability prescribed by the same convention. A certificate of insurance in the form presented by the convention must be carried on board and available for inspection at all times by any 'competent authority'.

So far as the UK is concerned, the clubs assist their oil-carrying members by providing a 'blue card' which provides the documentary evidence needed for a tanker owner to obtain the internationally required certificate of insurance. The blue card merely satisfies the existence of a policy of insurance (i.e. P & I cover in respect of oil pollution liabilities, in particular CLC liabilities) and the period of time for which the period of cover is effective.

An interesting insurance situation arose as a result of the enlarging of the wording contained in clause 1 of the Lloyd's Open Form of Salvage Agreement in its 1980 revised version. A fresh provision was included to the effect that salvage contractors who voluntarily provided their services to aid a stricken cargo-laden tanker in distress but failed in their attempt should nevertheless be guaranteed 15% of their outlays (known as the 'safety net' provision). This forms an exception to the traditional basis of the LOF that 'no success means no reward' or, as printed at the head of the form, 'no cure no pay'. There were those who attempted to argue for the creation of a fourth form of salved property (i.e. 'pollution liability') and thus persuade the clubs to accept money awarded in that respect. But such a form of 'property saved' was so hypothetical and impossible of financial definition that an argument based on such a theory was doomed to attract few backers and indeed it did not. Hull underwriters naturally accepted that it was they who must pick up the tab for the saving of hull and machinery, and cargo underwriters for the saving of cargo. But there was much discussion between those interests and the P & I clubs and liability underwriters as to who should be properly concerned in the 'grey' area of the 'safety net' payment and the enhancement of the awards for traditional property saving where there had been a merited degree of pollution avoidance in the same salvage operation. What emerged from these discussions (in 1980) was a so-called 'funding agreement' between the International Group of P & I clubs and the Institute of London Underwriters (ILU) and Lloyd's Underwriters Association that in consideration of the clubs providing security for and bearing the full cost of the 'safety net' provisions in clause 1 of the revised LOF for loaded or partly loaded tankers, the respective market underwriters would accept for their account salvage awards for the respective properties saved *including* the enhancement, if any was awarded by arbitrators or courts for merited efforts in avoiding escape of or pollution by oil.

Collisions

Historically, this risk has pride of place in the list. Hull cover has traditionally extended only to 3/4 of the damages payable to other vessels or other third parties, e.g. the owner of cargo carried in the other 'vessel'. The origin of this lay in a High Court ruling of 1836 that a hull policy did not cover at all damage caused by the assured's vessel to other vessels or third parties. Following this ruling an additional cover was designed by market underwriters which became known as the running down clause (see now the 3/4ths collision liability clause). It was this clause which extended cover to include 3/4 of collision liabilities but at the same time excluded altogether liabilities arising from death or injury, cargo damage or loss—for cargo on the assured's vessel—and wreck removal. The thinking behind this creation of the underwriters of those days was that to deny the assured the final 1/4 recovery would instill in him at least some measure of will to 'drive' with due care and attention. The assumption at that time was that the owner would remain self-assured for that last 1/4 but with the extent and value of liabilities increasing even 1/4 became more than the average owner could reasonably bear for his own account and it was by associating together to mutually insure each other against this 1/4 risk that shipowners formed the mutual clubs. (About three years ago the clubs who formed the International Group initiated the idea of extending P & I cover to include all collision liability and not merely the 1/4 not covered by the hull market. Clearly the guiding factor as to whether such a change could reasonably be made would be a comparison between what would be the increase in P & I calls and the corresponding decrease in hull premiums. From an administrative point of view there would be little change involved in that the club managers under the traditional arrangement of the 1/4–3/4ths split often take on the entire claims handling and the negotiating of settlements and/or engaging of lawyers as the case may be. This is because the P & I underwriter is the largest single underwriter over the entire insurance cover, since the 3/4ths portion covered by the hull market would usually be split over several underwriting interests, none of whose share would likely be as big as the P & I underwriter's. The situation now is that it is up to each individual club as to whether it wishes to continue offering the traditional 1/4th collision liability cover, or whether it will offer 4/4ths and thus bring collision liability 100% into its 'fold'.)

How is liability apportioned as between the vessels? Where one vessel *only* is to blame or where neither vessel is to blame there are no problems. In the former case the market underwriter of the assured vessel (which is liable) will reimburse 3/4 of the claim lodged by the wholly innocent vessel and the club will reimburse the remaining 1/4 subject to any deductible. The market underwriters' 3/4 portion will be subject to a ceiling of the declared value of the vessel. In the latter case where neither vessel is to blame there is no liability anyway and therefore each vessel bears its own loss.

However, in the vast majority of situations, both ships are to blame (or even more if it is a multiple collision) in whatever degree of fault. The UK is a 'convention' country—the 1910 Convention on Collisions and Salvage was ratified by the UK's Maritime Conventions Act and brought into force by 1911. Under this Act the adjustment in law is that although each vessel has a liability to the other to pay damages in proportion to her degree of fault, there is only in practice a *single* liability, i.e. the greater to the lesser, the greater's liability being to pay the difference between the two sums.

Simple and logical though this rule of law may be, underwriters could be disadvantaged by applying this method of the one single payment. They, therefore, made it a term of the policy of hull insurance that adjustment should be made on the basis of *cross*-liabilities, that is to say treating each vessel's liability to pay damages to the other as a separate process without the lesser liability being set off against the greater.

The following are examples of a settlement based on, first, a single liability and, secondly, on cross-liability.

(a) Settlement based on single liability

The vessels *Alpha* and *Beta* are involved in a collision, both vessels being equally to blame. *Alpha* is damaged in the sum of £40,000, *Beta* is damaged in the sum of £20,000, the aggregate liability is £60,000.

The vessels are liable in proportion of 50%, i.e. £30,000. As *Alpha* has suffered £40,000 in damage but needs to bear only £30,000, *Beta* must pay to *Alpha* £10,000. For the shipowners the effect is that the owner of the *Alpha* has suffered damage to the sum of £40,000 but receives £10,000 from the owner of the *Beta* and suffers, therefore, an overall loss of £30,000. The owner of the *Beta* has suffered damage in the sum of £20,000 but has also to pay £10,000 to the owner of the *Alpha* and suffers, therefore, an overall loss of £30,000.

The owner of the *Alpha* will claim £40,000 from hull underwriters for the damage suffered by his vessel and his hull underwriters will be subrogated to his claim against the owner of the *Beta* for £10,000. Hull underwriters' total liability will, therefore, be in the sum of £30,000. The owner of the *Alpha* will have no claim against his P & I club.

As there is only one single liability between the owner of the *Beta* to the owner of the *Alpha*, the owner of the *Beta* will claim £20,000 from hull underwriters for the damage suffered by his vessel and 3/4 of his liability of £10,000 (i.e. £7,500) under the collision liability clause. The owner of the *Beta* will also have a claim for 1/4 of his liability to *Alpha* (i.e. £2,500) on his P & I club.

(b) Settlement based on cross-liability

Assuming that the same collision occurs between the same vessels and both vessels have the same fault and suffer the same amount of damage, the settlement based on the principle of cross-liabilities will be as follows: *Alpha* will owe 50% (i.e. the proportion of claim) of *Beta*'s damage (i.e. £20,000) which amounts to £10,000. *Beta* will owe 50% (i.e. the proportion of blame) of *Alpha*'s damage (i.e. £40,000) which amounts to £20,000.

The difference actually payable by the owner of the *Beta* to *Alpha* will be £10,000, i.e. the same as under a settlement according to single liabilities. Under this system, however, there are two claims, *viz*, *Alpha* against *Beta* and *Beta* against *Alpha* and the rules of subrogation come into play on both sides so that there will be a difference in the involvement of the respective insurers.

The owner of the *Alpha* will claim £40,000 from hull underwriters in respect of the damage suffered by his vessel plus 3/4 of his liability (i.e. £10,000) to *Beta* (i.e. £7,500). The owner of *Alpha*'s total claim against his hull underwriters is, therefore, £47,500. Hull underwriters, however, will be subrogated to *Alpha*'s claim against *Beta* (i.e. £20,000) so that the total liability of the hull underwriters will be £27,500. (Under settlement based on single liability the total liability of hull underwriters was in the sum of £30,000.) The owner of *Alpha* will have a claim against his P & I club for 1/4 of his liability (£10,000) which is £2,500. (Under settlement based on single liability the owner of *Alpha* had no claim against his P & I club.)

The owner of *Beta* will claim £20,000 from hull underwriters in respect of the damage suffered by his vessel plus 3/4 of his liability (i.e. £20,000) to *Alpha* (i.e. £15,000). The owner of *Beta*'s total claim against his hull underwriters is, therefore, £35,000. Hull underwriters, however, will be subrogated to *Beta*'s claim against *Alpha* (i.e. £10,000) so that the total liability of the hull underwriter will be £25,000. (Under settlement based on single liability the total liability of hull underwriters is in the sum of £27,500.) The owner of *Beta* will have a claim against his P & I club for 1/4 of his liability (£20,000) which is £5,000. (Under settlement based on single liability the owner of *Beta* had a claim against his P & I club for £2,500.)

In addition to the one-quarter collision, the clubs give protection against the exposure to *excess* liability. In simple terms, this means that if a small ship with only a modest insured value collides with and heavily damages a much larger ship thus incurring collision liability very disproportionate to its own insured value, the clubs will accept that balance over and above the three quarters of insured value which is the limit placed by hull underwriters on their own liability to pay out collision damages under the hull policy. One proviso to this cover being provided, however, is that the insured vessel must be insured for its realistic value. The vessel must, in other words, not be under-insured.

Club rules contain what is known as a 'sister ship' clause which provides that where the entered vessel has been in collision with another vessel belonging either wholly or partly to the member, the member shall be entitled to recover the same amounts from the club and the club shall have the same rights as if such other vessel belonged wholly to different owners. For example, where ship (A) collides with ship (B) then the owner of ship (B) is entitled to recover for the damage sustained by his vessel from hull underwriters as a loss by perils of the sea. Having settled this claim under the hull policy, the insurers on hull are then subrogated to the rights of the assured shipowner and become entitled to proceed against the owner of ship (A) in respect of his proportion of fault in causing the collision. Where, however, ships (A) and (B) are under the same ownership, the hull insurers, standing in the shoes of the owner of ship (B) will find that they are unable to take legal action against the owner of ship (A) on the principle that no person can take legal action against himself. So as to remedy this situation, hull insurance conditions were introduced which provided that the assured should have the same rights under his policy as he would were the other vessel entirely the property of owners not interested in the vessel, so that the subrogated insurers would be capable of recovering from the guilty ship. Similarly, a sister ship clause has been inserted in P & I cover to provide for a member to be indemnified in respect of the sums he has to pay in respect of his vessel at fault and also in respect of a loss for which he would have been liable had the other vessel belonged to another person. Also, the insurers of ship (B) would escape their liability for the collision because they would not have been called upon to indemnify the owner of ship (B) because he would not have been sued by himself.

Exposure to collision liabilities is greater under American law/jurisdiction than it is under English jurisdiction or any other jurisdiction which has adopted the Collision Convention of 1910. Under the Convention those ships involved in a collision (and the word 'involved' should be particularly noted because it is very possible to have liability for a collision without actually making a physical contact) are only liable for the damage/loss they cause to the other ship or their cargoes in the same proportion as is their degree of fault. It has been said that a third-party cargo-owner is 'tainted' with the same guilt as the ship which is carrying his own cargo. Thus, under the Convention a third-party cargo-owner whose cargo is lost or damaged can only recover from each shipowner, who is partly at fault for the collision, that portion of the damages for which that ship is at fault. Under US law (and the USA never ratified the 1910 Convention) the third-party cargo-owner is an 'innocent' party untainted with the guilt of the carrying vessel and is free to sue either vessel for his full 100% damages regardless of the proportion of fault of either. He will generally be unable to recover from the carrying vessel because of the terms and conditions of the contract of carriage which afford to the carrying owner the defence of negligent navigation. The prudent cargo-owner, under US law, will seek full recovery from the non-carrying vessel who will in turn seek a contribution under the rule of mutual contribution between joint tortfeasors. Thus a carrying vessel owner can find himself exposed, in a collision situation in which he himself is partly to blame in whatever degree, to paying out collision damages to the owners of the cargo on board his own ship by the way of payment circuitously via a contribution to the other non-carrying partly to blame ship where if sued directly by that same cargo-owner he would have a full and firm defence under the printed conditions of carriage. This anomalous situation was rectified to some extent by the introduction of the 'both to blame collision clause' which purported to entitle the carrying owner to seek back from his shipper the contribution which he has been obliged to pay out to the other ship.

So, under US jurisdiction the scenario for exposure of involved ships to cargo claims following a collision is similar to the scenario for death/personal injury claims under the convention, i.e. the claimant may sue either ship for full damages and then the ships will adjust as between themselves according to their respective degrees of fault.

What happens when the US and a Convention jurisdiction become involved in litigation arising from one collision was tested in the case of *The 'Giacinto Motta'* (1977), where the third-party cargo claim (against the non-carrier) was resolved in US jurisdiction and thereafter in English jurisdiction, the non-carrier sought to recover 50% of what he had paid out to the US third party from the carrier. This latter action had the effect of testing the efficacy of section 1(1)(c) of the British Maritime Conventions Act 1911. It was found to be effective, allowing the carrying vessel the same protection under the contract of carriage of goods by sea against the other vessel seeking recovery by way of indemnity as it did against the cargo-owner direct.

Thus, P & I protection does not appear to be required for this type of action except in US jurisdiction where owners can be obliged to pay out contributions and when the protection of the both to blame collision clause is outlawed as being against public policy.

As regards those risks which are wholly excluded from the running down clause (RDC) the club offers full 4/4 coverage: (1) raising, removal of wrecks; (2) any real or personal property except other ships or vessels and property on other ships or vessels; (3) pollution or contamination.

Non-contact damage

More colloquially known as 'wash' damage, this is the type of incident where one ship can cause physical damage to another without making actual physical contact with it. An obvious example is where one ship is moored at a river berth and another proceeding up or down river at an excessive speed, passes unnecessarily close to the berthed ship and creates rough water which causes the berthed ship to range up and down against its berth with the result of damage not only to it but possibly also to the berth itself. The moving vessel could be held liable in negligence both to the moored vessel owners and to the berth owner under the ordinary principles of tort law, providing, of course, that negligence can be proved against her.

Another example of non-contact damage would be if ship (A), by executing a negligent manoeuvre, caused ship (B) to run aground. Again no contact, but a fault is committed causing damage. The negligent manoeuvre of ship (A) might cause two other ships (B) and (C) to collide in which case all three ships (A), (B) and (C) would be 'involved' in a collision within the meaning of the Collision Convention (section 1 of the Maritime Convention Act 1911).

Some clubs are vague in their printed rules. Some clubs have a clear collision rule but have no rule specifically directed to non-contact damage. Such clubs may have a rule which follows the collision rule and deals with 'property not on board an entered ship'. The wording of such rules generally gives no hint as to how or why such loss/damage might be caused and it can only be assumed that non-contact, e.g. wash, damage, would come under it. Other club rules, however, are clear and specific, and provide specifically for 'non-contact damage to ships' which covers liability for losses caused to any other ship or cargo or other property therein.

Life salvage

Salvage reward for saving life alone is not payable under general maritime law though there are statutory provisions in the United Kingdom (Merchant Shipping Act 1894, section 544) making it obligatory. Thus, it is natural that hull and cargo underwriters do not customarily consider themselves obliged to indemnify their assured for such an expense. It is here that we find the clubs filling a gap in typical fashion but agreeing, to use the words of the rule itself, to indemnify for 'life salvage, not recoverable under the hull and machinery policies of an entered ship or from cargo-owners or underwriters'. Recovery under this rule by an owner member would be in circumstances where *only* life had been saved. Where life had been saved concurrently with property, recovery from the club would, it is thought, be dependent upon whether the enhancement to the property award for the saving of life was capable of separate calculation. If not, it would be up to the property underwriters to reimburse.

Stowaways/refugees

The clubs will reimburse their members for the expenses incurred in keeping stowaways on board until such times as they can be disposed of ashore and also with the cost of repatriating them to their country of origin as and when that can be arranged. In recent times the 'stowaways' rule has been used to accommodate a member whose ship has picked up boat people in South East Asia and has had to maintain them on board until such times as they can be disposed of, which is not always easy. Some club members have even put in a claim for demurrage for the delay incurred in a particular port (e.g. Hong Kong) whilst negotiations were conducted for the landing and receipt of the refugees into suitable facilities. Demurrage is an exclusion from club cover and this part of their claim would be denied.

Quarantine

Quarantine expenses are recoverable if incurred because of the outbreak of an infectious disease on board, including an order that a ship be disinfected. The club's liability is restricted to net expenses, that is to say after deductions of those costs or expenses which would have been incurred anyway despite the quarantine. The costs/expenses contemplated are bunkers, insurance, wages, stores, provisions and port charges.

Damage to fixed objects and floating objects

The word 'collision' tends to conjure up for the layman only mental pictures of ship hitting ship, not of ship hitting wharf, dock or pier. But that is just as much a collision in the general maritime law sense and indeed the injured wharf owner has a lien on the ship for the damage as do any of his employees who may have been injured in the incident. But insurance rules differ. As we have seen collisions between ships (and, more strictly, to use the relevant word in the Maritime Conventions Act 1911, *involving*) are covered to the extent of 1/4 of an assured's liability for the damage caused to the other ship(s). If an assured's vessel strikes and damages fixed property, the club bears the full risk because this sort of risk is excluded from the 3/4 collision liability clause in hull policies. It is, therefore, yet another example of the clubs having grown over the years on the basic premise that their purpose is to cover those risks which cannot be placed elsewhere in any other form of insurance policy. The wording of this particular rule generally refers to 'damage to any harbour, dock, pier, jetty, structure, buoy, submarine or other cable fixed or movable object including land or property thereon not being a ship'. The word 'movable' would presumably cover such objects as a shore crane running along a wharf. A buoy is not fixed in the sense of being rigid but is nevertheless a fixture and is clearly not a vessel.

One feature of the rules of a P & I club is that great care is taken to ensure that there is no duplication or overlapping between rules. For example, damage by oil pollution, if the object damaged is a wharf, could be said to come under the fixed object rule, but in fact all loss/damage resulting from pollution by oil comes under a separate (oil pollution) rule and has been described earlier in this chapter.

Cargo

The risks of loss or damage to cargo were added some time after the initial founding of the 19th century protection clubs. Indeed, it is not a 'protection' risk, it was the first of the 'indemnity' risks, since the risk of liability arose from the employment of the ship rather than from its ownership. Carriers of cargo, although hard pressed in those days by English common law (there was no relevant statutory law) which allowed them very few exceptions to what was otherwise strict liability, protected themselves not by insurance but under the law by inserting into their bills of lading as many protective clauses as they could. This they were entitled to do under the *laissez-faire* doctrine of freedom of contract. Thinking that they had thus sealed up any exposure they might have had to contractual liability and that their position was well-nigh impregnable, they were understandably dismayed and their confidence shaken when the *Westenhope* incident occurred in 1871 and the courts failed to protect an owner carrier whose vessel had been guilty of a deviation and cargo was lost/damaged as a result. They realised that protecting clauses in a contract of carriage were not necessarily overall protection from attack by cargo interests and that indemnity insurance was at the least advantageous, if not wholly necessary.

Club cover on cargo is now defined in club rules along the following lines:

> 'Loss or damage to or responsibility in respect of cargo or other property intended to be or being or having been carried in an entered ship for which the member may be liable, including claims for short delivery, unseaworthiness, improper stowage, defective or insufficient dunnaging or ventilation, heating, sweating, theft or pilferage, damage by contamination or leakage from other goods.'

Selecting a suitable illustration of a typical cargo claim handled by a club would be like trying to make a conscious decision as to which grain of sand to pick from a seashore. However, one which is typical perhaps both of the practicalities of sea carriage and the legal issues likely to be faced is this example.

A club-entered Turkish vessel was chartered for a single voyage to load urea in bulk at a Black Sea port for discharge at Antwerp. The vessel duly presented itself for loading. The shipper's surveyor took one look at the ship's six holds and pronounced them unfit for the carriage of the intended cargo. They were not just unclean, they were flaked or coated with rust throughout, some of it lumps as large as the palm of a man's hand. The master was recommended to clean the holds and in response to his request for cleaning assistance from ashore, he was told there was none. His crew spent the next 11 days cleaning and after three subsequent inspections had failed to pass them fit, on the fourth inspection they were declared fit. The cargo was loaded and perhaps it was not altogether unexpected that the urea was found on arrival to be heavily contaminated with rust particles. The discharge process itself further aggravated the contamination by reason of the grab dischargers knocking rust particles from the sides of the hold. The cargo was discharged into barges and in addition to the basic claim lodged for the rust contamination (apparently it is virtually impossible to derust urea effectively) the cargo receivers claimed for the barge hire during the post-discharge period when surveyors and other experts were doing their work. The total sum claimed was around US$1,200,000. One strange feature which investigations unearthed afterwards was the lack of any bill of lading covering the cargo. The shippers had never approached the master at the Black Sea end, but at Antwerp the relief master (they had changed mid-voyage) found himself facing a request to sign clean bills at the conclusion of what had turned out to be, for the cargo at any rate, a fatal voyage. Needless to say the master flatly refused.

The club managers, as they will without hesitation do if they consider that an outside double check on their own in-house legal expertise is worthwhile, sought counsel's opinion on whether a shipowner carrier was legally liable for cargo damage on the basis of failure to provide a seaworthy ship (or more accurately an uncargo-worthy ship) if the condition which renders it unfit was known, before loading, to the cargo shipper and he had, through his surveyor, indicated that the condition was remedied. The first opinion obtained was that there was a reasonable chance that such an argument would succeed and that the law would expect such a shipper/charterer to exercise his option to reject the ship and hire a substitute, thus making his provable loss merely the difference between what he had paid by way of freight for that ship and what he would have had to pay for the use of a substitute, assuming he could have got one and assuming there was such a difference. Investigations in fact showed that on that theory, the cargo's losses would have been around $100,000. Efforts to settle by splitting the difference between the amount claimed and $100,000, i.e. for not exceeding $600,000, failed. Cargo's solicitors displayed such a dogged insistence that their client be compensated his full amount, that the club double checked on their double check by taking a further counsel's opinion, which was that nothing can displace the absolute duty to furnish a seaworthy vessel when presenting it for loading under a charter-party. Once accepted and the cargo loaded, the shipowner must face the consequences of the unseaworthy condition, subject to any exceptions he might have in his favour in the charter-party.

The claim was eventually compromised at $900,000. All this happened in the first half of the 1980s.

Restrictions of scope of cargo cover

Terms of contract of carriage

A restriction on members whose vessels carry cargo is that the contracts of carriage into which the member enters from time to time with shippers should be on terms no less favourable to him than the Hague (or Hague-Visby) Rules. Typical wording which you could expect to find in a club's rule book is:

'Provided that unless the association has agreed or arranged cover on special terms (which may include the requirement of additional call or premium) or unless the committee in its sole discretion shall otherwise determine, there shall be no recovery in respect of liabilities, costs or expenses which would not have been incurred by the member if the contract of carriage had been subject to the Hague Rules or the Hague-Visby Rules, except and to the extent that such are overridden by other rules, conventions or provisions of national or international law which may mandatorily apply.'

This wording is sufficiently flexible in composition to include the Hamburg Rules if, as it seems now quite possible, they achieve international effect. For it should be understood that a cargo-carrying member's liabilities under the Hamburg Rules would be covered in the same way, although such liabilities would be increased. The insistence of the clubs that their members who carry cargo for value should avail themselves of at least these minimum standards of legal protection (perhaps the most valuable legal defence afforded by the Hague-Visby code is the 'negligent navigation' defence (controversial though its continued existence is), is part of the general policy that they as the liability insurers should have the same protection as far as it is reasonably possible as the member himself, particularly in the area of limitation of liability.

The New York Produce Exchange Form of charter-party failed in its printed form to provide a clear expression of the division of responsibility for cargo claims between owner and charterer. To minimise disputes and more importantly to reduce to a minimum the costs and expenses of solving disputes (which is one of the fundamental objectives of any club) the clubs themselves which form the International Group came to an agreement between themselves known now worldwide as the Inter-Club Agreement. It contains a formula for the apportioning of responsibility for cargo claims, which was intended to forestall and replace the dispute-resolving process. The formula is as follows: claims for loss or damage to cargo due to unseaworthiness—100% owners. Claims for damage due to bad stowage or handling, including slacking/ullage—100% charterers. Claims for short delivery, including pilferage and overcarriage—50% owners/50% charterers.

The formula and the agreement within which it is contained only applies if the charter-party itself has not undergone a significant and/or material amendment. This would have to be a particularly definitive amendment such as to so clarify the respective liabilities as to make the formula totally unreflective in that particular charter-party of the respective intentions of the principal parties. It is, however, to be noted that the incorporation into the charter of an international code of rights and liabilities such as the Hague or Hague-Visby Rules would not have this definitive effect.

What would be regarded as a material amendment is the addition of the words 'cargo claims' in clause 26 as the cargo claims thereby would fall to be for owners' account. Such a charter-party, if so amended, would fall outside the application of the agreement. If, however, as is frequently found, the words 'and responsibility' are added in after the word 'supervision' in clause 8 making the master obliged to supervise *and* be responsible for stowage, the legal effect of those words being added causes the burden of legal liability for poor stowage to revert back from the charterer, where it naturally lies under the basic wording (which is unaffected by the mere word 'supervision') to the owner. If clause 8 is thus amended, the basic formula is altered to the extent that claims for bad stowage, bad handling, etc., are divided 50/50 and not attributed 100% to charterers' account.

Deviation

The clubs take the same 'abhorrent' view as the traditional marine insurance market regarding deviation from the contract voyage. Deviation, to make it that much more complicated, has two meanings in maritime law:

(a) A departure from the contractual voyage, i.e. a physical or geographical deviation from the insured voyage.

(b) A deviation from the contract of carriage which amounts to a flagrant breach, or perhaps almost abuse, of the terms and conditions of carriage.

Both forms of deviation are excepted from club cover for cargo liabilities. All clubs have a deviation rule which in simple paraphrase provides that there shall be no recovery in respect of claims which have arisen proximately as a result of a deviation from the contract voyage. This basic exclusion is, however, coupled with a proviso that if the member notifies the club in advance of his intention to deviate, the club may hold him covered at no extra cost, depending on the gravity or lack of it of the deviation, or alternatively may arrange on the member's behalf SOL (shipowners' liability) insurance cover for the deviation period. In practice the clubs maintain an open deviation cover on the market enabling them simply to declare each incident to the market insurers as and when the member gives notice. It is not surprising that the clubs, or indeed for that matter any marine insurers, are reluctant to condone deviation since in law it is regarded as a breach of contract so fundamental as likely to cause the removal of the right to limit liability available to the carrier under the terms and conditions of carriage embodied in the bill of lading.

The extent of the legal effects of a deviation varies according to the jurisdiction. Of the two jurisdictions of particular relevance in maritime claims, American courts will very probably deprive the offender of *all* his rights under the carriage contract including the right of package or unit limitation. England (being a Hague-Visby Rules country) will respect the wording of the Hague-Visby Rules which is that in any event (presumably meaning however heinous) the carrier will *not* be deprived of his right to limit per package or unit.

Turning to the second interpretation of the word 'deviation', to what extent does the club restrict cover? There are, of course, several practical examples of this sort of deviation of which the one that perhaps springs foremost to mind is the practice of placing goods (cargo) on deck and issuing under-deck bills of lading—on-deck space exposed to wind and weather being unacceptable (legally) as proper cargo-carrying space unless specifically agreed between carrier and shipper. That the club should bar recoveries in respect of any claim arising from such an event is natural for two reasons. First, it is a clear breach of the carriage agreement before the performance of carriage has even begun and, secondly, the issue of under-deck bills of lading is a deliberate falsification of a document of title and thus a fraudulent misrepresentation to those who might innocently purchase it.

Delivery without production of bill of lading

A third exclusion to cargo cover is when a member has thoughts of delivering cargo without production of the relevant original bill of lading. That the club should wish to exclude the risks to which an owner is exposed by doing this sort of thing is simply explained by the fact that the owner in taking on such a risk is deliberately incurring it and has calculatingly decided to give in to what is probably commercial pressure from the receiver, or rather the party who is claiming he is entitled to receive the goods. If this explanation fails to satisfy anyone then it could be equally argued in support of the club's policy that it would offend against the principles of mutuality to permit one member to follow a practice which was to his sole economic benefit and in so doing involve the club members who did not indulge in such self-gainful commercial practices.

The consequences of taking such a grave business risk (which is very different in nature to the range of accidental or fortuitous risks which the clubs cover) can be devastating, particularly where a high value oil cargo is concerned, for bearing in mind the way negotiable bills pass unseen from hand to hand as cargoes are bought and sold afloat, anyone could come along the next day and present a properly endorsed original. The red-faced shipowner and/or master is left facing a mammoth claim for misdelivery, will likely have his ship promptly arrested and will inevitably be faced with a large legal bill in attempting to extricate himself, the cost and expense of all of which he will be unable to seek back from the club. What the club managers can and will frequently do is to advise how best an owner member can secure himself against the possible adverse consequences and this will be to accept a letter of guarantee suitably endorsed by a reputable bank indemnifying the owner against any consequences of delivering the goods without production of the original bill of lading. The advice will also include a warning to insist that the amount of the guarantee is at least one and a half times the value of the cargo to cover the likelihood of the vessel being arrested and the incurring of heavy legal costs. It will be rare, if ever, that a bank will consent to give an open-ended guarantee without fixed limit.

False descriptions in bill of lading

A further restriction on club cover on cargo has reference also to bill of lading description. It is reasonably common practice for commercial reasons and to retain the good will of shippers for a carrier to turn a blind eye to cargo damage noted at the time of shipment and to issue bills of lading omitting to state its true condition. This, as in the case of stowing goods on deck and issuing under-deck bills, is a falsification of a legal document, upon the strength of the truth, on which other people rely and constitutes a deliberate misrepresentation. If a master on behalf of his owners does this to please a shipper or charterer then he should best protect himself by getting in return a letter of indemnity which will have at least some practical protection, though if it turns out at the end of the day that he wishes to enforce the indemnity letter he will find in the UK no court of law to support him because it has been held that no legal body can be seen to condone the validity of a letter given to induce somebody else to issue a fraudulent document. Certainly a club will have nothing to do with any claims arising from that cause.

The practice of ante- or post-dating bills of lading, although many would say that this is only a minor transgression, also forms an exclusion from club cover, though in practice the adverse consequences which do arise from this common habit would seem to be rare.

Refrigerated cargoes

Refrigerated cargo carriage receives special attention in the rules. Clearly the safe preservation of this type of cargo is dependent entirely upon the efficiency of the apparatus and the keeping of cargo spaces at a controlled and suitable temperature. The club therefore requires that the refrigerated cargo spaces and the apparatus are inspected just prior to the carrying voyage commencing. The managers may also require the member to give advance information as to the conditions of carriage, shippers' instructions for stowage, etc. Unless these preconditions are satisfied, the club reserves the right to deny the member any recovery from the club in the event of subsequent claims arising.

Irrecoverable general average

Basically this head of risk is defined simply as GA, or special charges which a member would be entitled to claim from cargo or cargo interests, but is prevented from doing so solely by reason of breach of the contract of carriage (e.g. a fundamental breach such as the unseaworthiness of the vessel). Such a breach entitles the cargo interests to refuse to pay general average contributions or similar charges.

Bearing in mind that P & I insurance is not intended to overlap in any way or at any point with any other form of insurance which the assured may have in respect of his marine risks, it is the practice of the clubs' managers to delete those items alluding to ships' sacrifices (properly the province of hull underwriters) before making reimbursement of irrecoverable general average to a member.

This can be a worry to P & I claims' adjusters who are dealing with this particular risk in that general average adjustments can contain a large number of items in respect of ship's sacrifice. Cargo interests in recent years have become increasingly reluctant to contribute to general average and will only do so under the greatest possible pressure. General average adjustments can take a number of years to complete and issue and at a late stage if ship's sacrifice items are still included in the general average adjustment and have not by that time been separated, an embarrassing situation can develop *vis-à-vis* the member's hull underwriters if they are required to reopen this aspect of their liability after so long a time. The claims adjusters are best advised, therefore, to ask the member to request his average adjuster at least to make an indication as to which amounts in the adjustment are referable to ships' sacrifices so that the member can know as early as possible what proportion of the general average will not be recoverable from the association/club in any event. Also it enables the member to put his hull underwriter on notice at the outset rather than at the 'eleventh hour'.

Ship's proportion of general average

Clubs indemnify members in respect of the entered ship's proportion of general average, special charges for salvage not recoverable under the hull policies by reason of the value of the ship being assessed for contribution to general average and salvage at a sound value in excess of the insured value under the hull policies.

A condition precedent to recovery under this item is that the club's committee may, for the purpose of assessing any sum recoverable under this head, determine the proper value which the entered ship should have been insured for under its hull policies and the club shall only pay the amount of the ship's proportion which would have not been recoverable under the hull policies even if the ship had been insured thereunder at such value. Just as with collision liability cover, when considering the 'proper value' for which an entered ship should be insured or deemed to be insured, the club's committee will require to be satisfied that the hull policies of the member have been the subject of periodic review as market conditions may require.

Towage contracts

Shipowners in the course of the daily trading of their ships often have reason to engage the services of a tug, e.g. for berthing or unberthing, manoeuvring within a port, or for towing a dead ship from one place to another. As early as the 1930s tug owners in the United Kingdom jointly devised a standard form of towage contract (UK STCS) which contained provisions and the legal relationship of tug and tow which included many indemnity clauses whereby the vast bulk of liabilities lay upon the tow owner. These terms were revised in 1974 and again in 1983 (the current terms). Following their policy of gradual extension of cover to meet new liabilities encountered by shipowners, the clubs accepted for cover liabilities arising under the 1974 UK Standard Conditions of Towage. The extent of the cover is as follows, paraphrasing a typical club rule: liabilities which a member may incur together with costs and expenses incidental to and arising out of a towage of an entered ship in the following situations: (a) under the terms of a contract entered into for the purpose of entering or leaving a port or for manoeuvring within that port whilst in the course of the vessel's ordinary trading activities. (b) Where an entered ship in the ordinary course of its trading is customarily towed from one port to another or from one place to another. A proviso to this second situation is that (i) the member should not already have insurance against these same liabilities under his policies on hull and (ii) that the ship should have been declared to the managers as being customarily under tow in that way. The third area of cover (c) is where the entered ship is under contract to be towed under terms other than the standard UK terms and conditions of towage. In that situation, for cover to be effective, the contract must have been already approved by the managers and the member should have paid, or should have agreed to pay, any additional calls or premium as the association may require from him.

Conversely, the clubs will cover a member where his ship undertakes the towage of another vessel and in doing so incurs liabilities. There are three provisos to this particular item of cover and these are (1) that where an entered ship is specially designed or converted for the purpose of towage it shall have been declared as such to the managers at the time of entry or at the time of conversion for the purpose of towage. And (2) the towage contract should have received the approval of the managers and the member should have paid or have agreed to pay any additional call or premium which may be required of him or (3) the committee in its discretion, after having been told of all the circumstances, should consider the terms of the towage contract as being reasonable and the liability arising from it as coming within the general scope of the cover given by the association.

Wreck of the entered vessel

The wording of this ruling includes the sequence of words: 'costs or expenses relating to the raising, removal, destruction, lighting or marking of the wreck of the entered vessel . . .' but it emphasises that it is *only* 'when those listed activities are compulsory by law or the costs of the same are legally recoverable from the member'.

A member is also covered against liabilities he may incur from the presence or involuntary shifting of the wreck or as a result of failure to remove, destroy, light or mark such a wreck, or even a liability because of the escape of oil from the wreck.

The club accepts its liability where the wreck became a wreck outside the vessel's period of insurance with the club but only where the casualty or event which caused the vessel to become a wreck occurred during the vessel's period of entry with the club. The club will continue to bear liability for wreck liabilities notwithstanding that other aspects of club cover have terminated because of sale or loss.

The value of stores, materials and the wreck itself saved shall first be deducted from a member's claim under this rule.

There shall be no recovery if a member has beforehand transferred his interest in the wreck other than by abandonment to his hull insurers.

Sue and labour expenses

Every P & I club under its ordinary cover will allow a member to recover extraordinary costs and expenses reasonably incurred after the occurrence of a casualty for the purposes of avoiding or minimising any liabilities, costs or expenses against which the member is insured within such ordinary cover. In evaluating the benefits which this particular rule may have to a member, account will be taken of any particular deductible figure which the member would have been obliged to have borne for his own account in any event.

Legal costs also may be recovered but only in so far as prior written notice may have been given to the club and the club in turn may have given approval of the same being incurred.

'Special direction of the committee' may seem self evident and indeed it is, so that if the committee actually directs that certain expenses be incurred in the interest of the member as a result of having exercised its sole discretion in the matter, such costs and expenses may be recovered.

There are certain costs which a shipowner, during the course of his trading activities may incur which could be viewed, depending upon your point of view, as either operational costs or as sue and labour costs and an example of these is the costs of tallying. Club managers are frequently asked by members whether they would accept for club account tallying costs on the ground that the employment of tally clerks is a measure taken in order to reduce the likelihood of shortage claims of packaged or pieced cargo. Although the borderline between what is an operational cost in this type of situation and what is a sue and labour expense is admittedly a very fine one, club managers tend to react to such a request by rejecting a member's approach for recovery of such expenses on the ground that tallying, like stevedoring, is an operational activity and the expenses of such a service are for the member's own account. It would, of course, be likely that club managers would agree to make arrangements for the provision of a tally service through the club representative at whatever port was involved, though the managers would no doubt make it very clear from the start that the costs of the service would be for the member's own account.

The omnibus rule

This provision of P & I cover, probably more than any other single feature of club cover, symbolises the uniqueness of P & I insurance and particularly the concept of mutuality—that insurer and insured are the same people and not on two different sides of the contractual fence. The omnibus rule is basically a 'sweep up' provision and symbolises the club attitude that if possible a member's claim should be brought within the cover even though it does not fall neatly into one of the specifically listed risks. This attitude is surely in marked contrast to the 'market' attitude that if a claim is not specifically mentioned in the strict terms of the policy it is excluded and no further questions need be asked nor approach made. The assured is expected to remain content with the policy's terms. The application of the omnibus rule is discretionary and it is the discretion not of the managers but of the committee of club directors which is exercised, which emphasises that the benefits of this rule must not be doled out indiscriminately but only to those who are genuinely deserving.

Another feature of the omnibus rule is that every time a claim is submitted for consideration under it, that claim is examined strictly on its own merits and not by reference to some similar set of circumstances which may have been presented for consideration at some earlier occasion. Claims must have arisen from incidents in the course of the management or operation of the member's ship or somehow be related to the business of owning, operating or managing vessels.

The omnibus rule also bears witness to the constantly changing nature of shipowners' risks and to the very development of the club cover itself. It was after all by reason of an unusual claim in the 1870s when a member sought indemnity for a liability to cargo which he had incurred by reason of a deviation, that the new indemnity class of cover in respect of cargo was born. In those days that deviation claim could probably have been initially considered under what we now know as the omnibus rule.

EXCEPTIONS AND LIMITATIONS TO CLUB COVER

Although cover, as has been explained, given by clubs within the International Group is unlimited with the one exception of the risk of oil pollution, there are exceptions, exclusions and limitations and what follows is devoted to listing and commenting upon them. Already it has been noticed under the cargo risk rule that what would have otherwise been widely spread cover is pruned heavily by various exclusions and limitations particularly in the special area of bills of lading.

Deductibles

Perhaps the first and most 'eye catching' form of limitation on club cover is the practice of imposing deductibles or initial amounts of money which are to be borne by the member for his own account in respect of any one claim settlement. There is more than one philosophy about the merits of the deductible system. There are some who say that the presence of a deductible, even though it may seem to the member to be an unwarranted 'blot on the landscape' of an otherwise attractively comprehensive insurance cover, is in fact a benefit, rather a more long-term one, to the member and will—in the long term—have the effect of lowering his overall insurance costs. Many members have many small value, routine claims against them and it is an inescapable administrative fact that a claim valued at $5,000 can generate as much paper work as a claim valued at $500,000. There are others who say that the imposition of a deductible has a deterrent effect and causes a member to be that much more cautious in conducting his trading operations with care and attention.

Deductibles are either set by the club (i.e. in the rules and are, as it were, 'across the board' for a particular type of claim) or at the instigation of the member when seeking either original entry into the club or seeking to renew his membership. In exchange for the acceptance of a deductible he may well negotiate for himself a favourable reduction in his advance call. Deductibles are not, of course, peculiar to P & I insurance, they are also to be found in the wider marine insurance—hull and cargo. What the deductible is to be distinguished from is the free of particular average warranty which means that the assured can claim reimbursement of the whole of his claim provided that the value of the claim has exceeded the amount warranty free.

A further distinction is between a 'franchise' and a 'deductible' in marine insurance terms. Franchise is that amount which must be exceeded before the insurer comes on risk at all and once it has been exceeded the insurer is liable (to his assured) for the whole amount of the claim *ab initio*. A deductible is that amount of the claim which the assured bears for his own account; above that the insurer indemnifies the assured with everything in excess.

Member's wilful misconduct

Clubs make no distinction between gross negligence and wilful misconduct and treat the former as being excluded from a member's right to a recovery just as much as the latter. All clubs expressly exclude liability to effect a recovery which is the direct consequence of an act of wilful misconduct. The standard of wilful misconduct is very closely inter-related to the taking of a commercial risk. If an owner has three or four different choices of action before him and chooses one which turns out to be right and successful he will have no problem, but if he chooses one which turns out sour then he has taken a bad commercial risk and should not expect to look to the club to reimburse him.

An interesting aspect of the difference in definition and effect of the standards of negligence on the one hand and wilful misconduct on the other is the comparison of similar behaviour standards which respectively, if flouted, cause the barring of limitation rights to an owner or anyone with an interest in a ship, e.g. a charterer. The 1957 Limitation Conventions (now replaced as of December 1986 by the 1976 'London' Limitation Convention), set the requirement that an owner or charterer, etc., in order to be entitled to the privilege of limiting his liability, must prove that the liability arose from an act or omission which occurred without his 'actual fault or privity'. Fault needs little explanation. 'Privity' means, in rough definition, knowledge or constructive knowledge which someone has and deliberately conceals, resulting in some accident, or fails to impart to someone else who could have usefully used it if he had had it. The 1976 Convention has introduced the new standard in its 'break clause' of reckless conduct heedless of whether loss or harm may result. How do these standards of conduct barring limitation (in law) weave into the rules of a P & I club offering liability insurance (unlimited) cover and being governed in basic terms by the Marine Insurance Act 1906? A case in point here is *The 'Eurysthenes'* (1976), the facts being that a club entered vessel had been sent to sea in an unseaworthy state with the prior knowledge and concurrence of the assured member such as to debar him from limiting his liability.

The club argued that such privity also debarred the member from the right of recovery from the club. But the club was on 'weak ground', for an accusation merely that the member's personal negligence or privity had contributed to the accident which gave rise to the liability upon which limitation was sought, was inconsistent with and not up to the level of unreasonable conduct which the club rules specifically lay down as the 'breaking' standards for denying cover. Some clubs have a rule which expects a member at *all times* (both before, during and after a casualty) to take such steps as a reasonable uninsured person would take. This must, it is submitted, contemplate a standard of behaviour over and above the merely negligent or 'omitting to do' level and be more in the realms of intentional or wilful conduct (whether reckless or not is something else again).

So long as the 1957 Limitation Convention ruled internationally, the standard of what (a) broke a shipowner's (or other's) right to limit and what (b) allowed a club to avoid making recovery to its member, were radically different. Under the 1976 Convention, they are very much on a par meaning that clubs will be faced with the unpleasant task of deciding whether to try to enforce their unreasonable conduct rules to deprive a shipowner of insurance cover in respect of a claim for which he is unable to limit his liability. The 1976 convention has the added attraction for the clubs that insurers of liability have the right in themselves to limit but this in turn raises the delicate question of can they limit if the member they are covering has himself exhibited conduct which denies him limitation? Or if this is not the criterion, can they (the insurers) plead all the defences against their member which they may have under either (a) the policy or (b) under statute?

Statistics currently witness that claims in respect of loss or damage to cargo form the largest aggregate for one type of claim under P & I cover. Some years ago personal injury and/or death claims 'topped the bill', largely due to the massive jury awards pouring forth from the United States courts. The reason for cargo claims overtaking them is probably the steep rise in values of bulk commodities and also the continuance in sheer volume of minor claims of a routine nature.

Cargo risks were not covered in the very early days of the protection clubs. Now the scope of the cover afforded in respect of cargo may be described as liabilities or unrecoverable expenditure together with costs or expenses connected with such liabilities in respect of cargo intended to be, being or having been carried in an entered ship arising out of a breach of a member's obligations or duties as a carrier of those goods or by any persons for whose acts, neglects or defaults the member is vicariously liable. Such cover includes claims for short delivery, short contents, damage, deterioration, contamination or any form of loss due to unseaworthiness, poor stowage (including bad or short dunnaging) or bad ventilation. Delay in delivery has become a loss also covered by the clubs under this cargo rule, this being due to judicial decisions and the coming into international prominence of the Hague-Visby update of the Hague Rules which equates delay together with loss and damage as a form of loss for the reasonable avoidance of which a carrier of goods has minimum inescapable obligations.

The rise in popularity in the last two years of the Hamburg Rules foretells the likely increase in the burden of cargo claim recoveries, for the Hamburg code is more of a shippers'/receivers' 'delight' and a carriers' 'nightmare' than either the Hague or Hague-Visby Rules. It lays down an 'across the board' criterion for liability of the carrier that he is presumed at fault unless he (the burden of proof being on him) proves otherwise, clearly widens the scope for successful cargo claims against him. However, the clubs have no intention of 'walking away' from Hamburg liabilities if and when they come in 'wholesale proportions'.

Perhaps more than in respect of any other type of claim, the clubs in the interest of their membership keep a tight control on the circumstances from which cargo claims are likely to arise. We have seen how one condition of a recovery by a member from the club is that that member has contracted for the carriage of goods on terms no less favourable to him than the Hague (or Hague-Visby) Rules. A second restriction on cargo cover is that no claim will be recoverable if the liability originally arose as a result of a deviation. Deviation in this sense is geographical and is a departure by the ship from the contract route. A deviation of this nature unless justified (under the common law) or considered reasonable (as allowed by the Hague or Hague-Visby Rules) is regarded as a fundamental breach going straight to the root of the contract and has the effect of depriving the carrier of any defences and exceptions he may have under the contract. Club rules are clear on these circumstances. A member's cover is excluded in the event of a deviation unless he has given the club prior notice of the intended deviation to enable the club to hold him covered with or without an additional premium. Most clubs have open cover on the market which can be simply endorsed as each instance is notified.

One perhaps strange extension (as opposed to restriction) on club cover in respect of cargo is to be found in all the group clubs' rules and is sub-titled 'member's own cargo'. This rule gives a member the right, where the cargo belongs to himself, to recover from the club in respect of any claim on that cargo to the extent only that no such recovery could be had if the cargo had belonged to a third party and to the extent only that the loss or damage is not recoverable under any other insurance on the same cargo. The origins of this rule are shrouded in mystery since, on the face of it, it seems to be an exception to the general principle that P & I insurance is third-party liability insurance and the situation contemplated by this rule is where a member has a liability to himself which is lacking in logic. It could be that in the days when P & I rules were being fashioned and were growing up, the members themselves were having a greater hand in the formation of the rules and of the cover which they were mutually fashioning for themselves and it also may be because there were far more examples of shipowners or part shipowners carrying their own cargoes and therefore having a need for this type of cover and perhaps finding it difficult under certain circumstances to place cargo insurance cover on the ordinary market. Whatever the origins of the rule may be, it is unlikely these days that the rule will be invoked, particularly where it is worded to the effect that only if there is no other insurance on the cargo can a member take advantage of the rule.

Damage to the entered ship

P & I insurance is not property insurance. To cover physical loss or damage to the vessel would be duplicating hull insurance and encroaching upon the hallowed cloisters of the proprietary marine market. An exception to this is the cover given by the charterer's club to their members' entered vessels. Physical loss or damage to the vessel caused by an incident which can be attributed to the charterer's fault or breach (e.g. damage through a breach of the safe berth clause in a charter-party or damage to a vessel caused by stevedores engaged by charterers and for whose negligence the charterer is legally liable) is covered by the rules of the charterer's club in its liability class (class II) but that is because viewed from the charterer's point of view that is a liability situation though not admittedly so much a third-party as a 'second'-party circumstance.

Equipment on board

This includes containers, stores, lashings, fuel. For the reasons given above, a member's own property is his to insure under some form of property insurance. He cannot look to his club.

Demurrage or delay to entered ship

This is an area where an assured is very much on his own, be he an owner or a charterer. Contractual demurrage is an arrangement worked out, calculated, agreed and inserted as a provision in a charter-party before a voyage even commences. It is thus an affixed and agreed penalty payment to cover a foreseeable situation—eventual delay. That is a very different concept to what is the natural concept of something insurable—a loss or damage arising from the happening of an event occurring with or without fault being involved. Demurrage is liquidated damages, not damages assessed in the light of the occurring of a happening after the insurance has been placed. It comes, therefore, under the category of a commercial risk not only taken but actually guarded against and provided for before the event takes place and the penalty is invoked.

Hire

Hire is not recoverable from a P & I club. An owner who seeks to cover himself against the risk of not being able to recover hire payment from his charterer can look to a specialist club.

Cancellation of charter

Losses arising from this cause again fall into the category of 'business risks' which are taken with 'eyes open' and are akin to bad debts, insolvency and bankruptcy. Not so much owners, but frequently charterers, are anxious to know that they can obtain cover against the likelihood of a shipowner, ship operator or ship manager going bankrupt. This is neither a traditional nor a logical P & I risk. The financial collapse of a party is a business event but not an event routinely to be found during and associated particularly with the operation of a vessel or the course of its daily life. Advice to a charterer seeking cover or guidance would be to double check on the credibility, reliability and financial integrity of the person or company with whom he intends to enter into a commercial contract with a well-known professional body, e.g. the Baltic Exchange or the International Maritime Bureau.

Salvage operations

There has been an understandable reluctance on the part of clubs to accept into membership salvors for those liabilities which spring from their activities as professional salvors rather than from their activities as traditional tug owners. This reluctance springs from respect for the pooling agreement and the desire not to inflict upon pool members claims of a significant size and a non-traditional nature. The leading case of *The 'Tojo Maru'* (1971), which achieved worldwide renown for the issues which it raised, was a disturbing example in the early 1970s of the liabilities which a professional salvor could incur during a salvage operation due to a negligent act of one of his employees. In *The 'Tojo Maru'* incident the salvage tug, the entered vessel of one of the clubs, was irrelevant to the salvage operation in that the tug itself caused no damage nor was the employee who committed the negligent act on board or even near the tug at the time. Very considerable damage was done to the already crippled *Tojo Maru* by an act of salvage negligence and the club concerned felt itself unable to accept that liability under its ordinary cover. It is, therefore, hardly surprising that modern club rules should specifically exclude liabilities arising directly from operations in which an entered ship may engage such as salvage, successful or attempted, drilling, dredging, pile driving or pipe laying.

It would be, however, very probable that a tug owner who did engage in salvage operations might be able to persuade his club to endorse the certificates of entry for his tugs to the effect that for (1) damage done by the entered vessel and (2) any act or omissions of persons aboard the entered vessel during salvage operations, cover would be extended, so excluding salvage operations only as and when the salvage tug was not an integral part of the salvage operation.

A similar attitude would likely be taken towards a dredger as an entered ship, where there would be a reluctance to open up the exposure of the pool and the International Group excess reinsurance underwriters to such specialised professional negligence as might be found in a dredging operation. A club might override the dredging exclusion and reinstate club cover by an appropriate endorsement on the certificate of entry.

PROPOSALS TO PLACE AN OVERALL LIMIT ON CLUB COVER

Views as to whether a fixed limit should be placed on P & I club cover or whether it should remain as it is now, without limit with the exception of oil pollution claims, are sharply and strongly divided, the division being almost equal. Eight of the 15 clubs which form the 'group' favour placing a limit, the others favouring the continuing of unlimited cover. However, in tonnage terms the eight represent 69.5% of the total tonnage. So the question is unlikely to be resolved in the foreseeable future unless support for one or other lobby becomes much more one-sided.

It will be of value, however, to run through briefly the arguments on either side. First, in favour of limit, it is said that there is an inherent wrong in the clubs professing to offer their members unlimited cover when they are by no means certain that they can meet a claim which by the excess loss limit at present lies at 1,000 million, and it is not wholly unthinkable that a claim could exceed even this amount. The balance would have to be collected by dipping into reserves and buffer funds and by way of supplementary calls from mutual members, and such a balance, even spread over a wide membership, could prove a problem to collect, especially as it would be additional to the normal calls payable over that year. It would be entirely within the bounds of possibility that the club on whose shoulders the primary liability falls might be unable to pay and might expose itself to being forced into liquidation either by its own member or by third-party claimants. This would be a disaster not only for that club but also for the reputation and general prestige around the world of the clubs as a whole. Such a loss of confidence could spell the demise of the P & I insurance system.

Alternatively, the anti-limit lobby argue that as the clubs basically cover their members' legal liability, the extent of that liability hangs to a great degree on the limit of liability set by law within the jurisdiction of the dispute. Cover, as provided to members on their liability may be ultimately determined and fixed by law. That in itself is a limit and the fact that it is not represented by an 'across the board' sum of money as a maximum does not make it unrealistic. To impose a limit (and what is contemplated would probably be considerably in excess of the excess loss reinsurance maximum) would have at least three effects: (a) it would set a figure at which claimants with catastrophic claims would set their sights and thus tend unrealistically to inflate the value of their claims. (b) It would weaken the strength and value of the shipowner's or charterer's right to limit liability (e.g. under the 1976 Convention) because it would set a figure which legislators would see as the 'sum assured' and to which they would strive to aim in the course of their future efforts to revise upwards the limits of liability provided by the Convention. At worst, there would be a worldwide move to abandon limitation altogether, whereas arguably the wiser move in these times is to do just the opposite and to give strong support to the Convention on limitation particularly now that it gives shipowners greater protection than ever before in their efforts to obtain the right to limit (i.e. because of the substitution of the reckless conduct rule for the former actual fault or privity concept). (c) A fixed limit could frighten reinsurers and have the effect of collapsing the market. They might see it as an admission that we were entering an era where catastrophic claims were the norm, that the risk of them was a reality and not, as at present, a fairly remote possibility.

5
CLAIMS AND CLAIMS HANDLING

THE CONDUCT OF CLAIMS

The role of the P & I club in relation to claims is of extreme importance and has increased dramatically over the years. On the occurrence of a casualty or similar accident being an insurance or potential insurance event the claims handling service of the club will inevitably be brought into operation.

It is an essential aspect of the service that clubs provide that they can counsel and advise their members, appoint lawyers and surveyors for them and arrange security for the release of vessels that may be arrested or threatened with arrest in particular situations.

Indeed, one of the unique and principal advantages to be gained from membership of a P & I association is the service which will be provided by the club managers through a superior claims handling operation. Although, strictly, it is the member himself who is in charge of handling claims that have been made against him, quite often, and particularly in the case of large claims, the P & I club will take over and handle practically all claims as regards their defence, negotiation and settlement.

It is therefore only in relatively rare instances, where, for example, there may be a conflict of interest between the club and its member, that the member himself will be required to handle the claim being made against him before making his claim for indemnity against his club.

It is quite common even where other insurers may be interested in the outcome of a particular claim that the club may nevertheless deal exclusively with that particular claim. This is very prevalent with the clubs' cover for collision liability.

We have stressed that the P & I clubs do fulfil a major role in claims handling but it must be made abundantly clear that their rules state in general that in circumstances where the club takes over the handling of any particular claim this does not imply any acknowledgement by the club or indeed any obligation of the club to pay any amount for which the assured may be held liable.

Depending on the size of the P & I association the majority of personnel employed are those engaged in claims handling. This is not surprising in view of the number and size of claims that will be handled by a club on a day-to-day basis. To assist them in this work P & I clubs have a worldwide network of representatives and correspondents who exist in order to assist club members who may be in difficulties in distant ports.

Any member who is confronted with a potential liability claim is expected to consult his P & I association, indeed he is required to do so by the club rules giving notice of any event likely to give rise to a claim which may affect the association.

P & I clubs put great importance on centralised control of claims and by this means they are able to discern very quickly new trends in the pattern of claims, thus ensuring that the members' interests are protected by taking appropriate measures at the earliest possible moment.

Once notice of a claim has been given by a member, the association assumes full conduct of the proceedings and appropriate action is taken and, depending on the merits of the claim, it is either settled, compromised or defended in arbitration or court proceedings. In any event there is extremely close consultation between the staff of a P & I association and the member concerned throughout. When a major casualty is involved this will sometimes require the attendance of a representative from the management or the agency staff on the spot in order that urgent important decisions can be taken with the minimum of delay.

The claims handling department of P & I associations is generally organised either on a departmental or syndicate basis. In circumstances where the syndicate system is operated, each member of the association is allocated to a particular syndicate, often based on the nationality of the vessel or maybe on geographical regions. The syndicate will be responsible for the various claims against the vessels allocated to it. In a situation where the managers of the association operate a departmental system the particular claim will be allocated to specialised departments, for example, there may be a cargo claims department, a crew claims department or an admiralty department. On occasions during the claims handling process it can become clear that the claim will most probably proceed to litigation and in this connection the club will normally put such a matter into the hands of independent lawyers.

The rules of most P & I associations provide that the managers have extensive discretionary powers related to claims handling procedures. The discretionary powers of the managers relating to the handling and settlement of claims generally include the right, if they so decide:

(a) to control or direct the conduct of any claim or legal or other proceedings relating to any liability, loss or damage in respect where of a member is or may be insured in whole or in part;
(b) to require the member to take any step in connection with the handling of such claim or proceedings which the managers may think appropriate;
(c) to require the member to settle, compromise or otherwise dispose of such claim or proceedings in such a manner and upon such terms as the managers see fit.

The powers available to the club to intervene are particularly extensive in view of the fact that the exercise of these powers is under no circumstances to be taken as being an admission of liability by the club. There is usually, furthermore, a rule which provides that if a member does not settle, compromise, dispose of or take steps in connection with the handling of the claim or proceedings as required by the managers in accordance with the direction of the managers, any eventual recovery by the member from the club in respect of such claim shall be limited to the amount he would have recovered if he had acted as required by the managers. Such would be an example of rules laid down by mainly United Kingdom-based P & I associations, whereas there is a somewhat different and more lenient approach taken in the rules of Scandinavian clubs. These provide that the club may take over the handling of claims made against their members only with the consent of the member. Nevertheless, even in these circumstances these clubs will adhere to the principle that this action does not imply that the association acknowledges any obligation to cover the liability which may be finally imposed on the member.

Such Scandinavian clubs normally provide that where the club has stated in advance and in writing that it will cover any liability that might be imposed on the member, then the club will always be entitled, regardless of the consent of the member, to take over the handling of the particular claim.

PAYMENT OF CLAIMS

The rules or articles of association of a P & I club provide a mechanism for payment of claims. It is the usual practice that once settlement has been achieved and the members have settled the claim directly with the claimant and put in their claim for reimbursement on the association that settlement will be effected direct to the member. It is usually the practice for all cheques to be signed by one member of the committee, that is by a director of the association, and then to be countersigned by the managers in the case of very large claims. For smaller cases it would be usual for the committee to give authorisation to the managers that their signature alone would suffice.

Other provisions in club rules can specify that in the case of compensation which is to be paid to a third party to cover a liability for which the club is liable to its member, it is to be effected by the club only against the receipt from the third party. Additionally another club rule relating to the payment of claims in general may state that in no case shall a member be allowed interest on any claim he may have against the club.

APPOINTMENT OF LAWYERS AND EXPERTS

A very important part of the clubs' claim handling facilities and provisions is that clubs universally give themselves power to appoint and employ, on behalf of the association, lawyers, surveyors or any other persons necessary for the purpose of dealing with any matter which may be liable to give rise to a claim by the member upon the club. These provisions state that the terms of employment of such lawyers or experts, although appointed on behalf of the member, should require them to report to and disclose information to the association, notwithstanding the fact that such information is otherwise the subject of privilege.

THE DUTIES OF MEMBERS AND CLUBS AS TO THE NOTIFICATION OF CLAIMS AND OTHER MATTERS

It is normal upon the occurrence of any casualty, claim or other event involving a member which may be liable to give rise to a claim on the association that the member must notify his club promptly of such an occurrence.

In general, such a rule is backed by a sanction that if the member fails in any way to fulfil these obligations then the P & I association committee or board of directors may in its discretion reject any claim arising out of the casualty or event or for that matter reduce the sum otherwise payable by the club. Some clubs do state that if a member fails in his obligations, the club will cover only such liability or loss as it would have had to cover had the obligations been fulfilled.

Normally, the club rules merely reflect the committee's power to reject the claim or to reduce it in quantum, whereas some of the older hull clubs and indeed modern non-marine insurers state that compliance with the condition of the policy with regard to notification of a potential claim is a condition precedent to a member's right to recovery. What may be considered to be a condition precedent must be regarded on the basis of pure construction.

The very important reason for the existence of such a rule by the club arises from the fact that P & I associations cannot make use of their rights of subrogation to contest the member's liability against a third party unless they first pay the assured the full amount of his loss. The rule reserves the club's right to conduct litigation in connection with the member's liability on his behalf.

Any delays, therefore, in a club being notified as to possible claims may well prejudice the club's ability to investigate the claim and consider alternative defensive arguments or indeed commence limitation proceedings.

A further reason for requiring notification of claims is, of course, to assist the club in maintaining adequate records. The underwriting department of a P & I association has to decide on call-rating on the basis of records over a period of time. These records are computed from information received from members regarding their claims submitted and claims about to be submitted.

As well as bringing into operation the claims handling process and making realistic calculations of premium it is important for a club to make an allocation of reserves to provide such a reserve in the case of potentially large claims. Therefore, this is another instance where prompt notification of possible claims is extremely important to the association. A further advantage of receiving prompt notification of claims is that it can assist the association's claims department to build up experience which will serve to the benefit of its members in the field of loss prevention.

Time at which the duty to notify claims to the club arises and methods of communication

Club rules do not generally define what is meant by a casualty or other event which may give rise to a claim against the association. In the majority of cases it will be quite obvious to the member as to what constitutes an event which may give rise to a claim but there are cases where there may be some doubt as to whether or not liability may eventually arise. There are many such cases, for example, where cargo can be damaged by water entering a hold through leaking hatch covers during a period of heavy weather. It is quite possible that such a leakage could be a direct consequence of the heavy weather and within the ambit of the Hague or Hague-Visby Rules. The exception of 'perils of the seas' may arise and, therefore, there may be no liability whatsoever attached to the carrier. Conversely, it may transpire that the leakage was caused by a defective hatch cover or the failure of the crew to properly close the hatch covers so that the vessel was unseaworthy at the inception of the voyage which would result in carrier's liability being involved. Of course, in these circumstances a member should notify the club of such an event even if the member is confident that no claim will arise against him for settlement by the club.

It is also of great importance to notify the club when a formal claim is made, even if the casualty has been reported earlier. In such circumstances the time factor will be of great importance to the club in handling the claim. Not only is the limitation period against the member of considerable importance but it may be that a claim is made against third parties who should be joined in the action and it also may be necessary for the club to arrange security for the release of the vessel if it has been arrested.

The duty to notify the club of a formal claim is presumably covered by the club provisions that a member must at all times promptly notify the managers of any information, documents or reports in his possession or knowledge to the casualty, event or matter. As the notification of a claim is of such importance it is perhaps unfortunate that the duty is, if the construction of this provision is correct, imposed by such an oblique provision and greater prominence could be given to the duty of the member.

There are two main aspects of great importance concerning the communication and notification of claims to the club. In the first place, how does a member notify the club of a casualty, and secondly, how does the club give notice to a member that it requires documents, surveys, statements or other investigation?

Most of the clubs have rules that specify, in greater or lesser detail, methods of giving the required notice to the club, one such example of these rules is as follows:

> 'A notice or other document required under these rules to be served on the association may be served by sending it through the post in a prepaid letter or by sending it by telegram, cable, radio telegraph or telex addressed to the association at the association's registered office for the time being.'

Notification to be communicated to the club is of extreme importance and the way in which most club rules are structured is that the obligation to notify is mandatory and that failure to do so gives the club committee the discretion to reduce or reject any claim which is eventually made against the club. This would appear to be the situation notwithstanding that the member's failure has in no way prejudiced the club's position.

What is not clear is whether a member's duty to notify is maintained in circumstances where the club has by other means already received notification of a potential claim. It may happen, for example, that an incident arises which gives rise to massive oil pollution or great loss of life which becomes readily apparent from the relevant public authorities or the world's press and becomes common knowledge. In these circumstances is the member still obliged to formally notify the club? Furthermore, when a club is informed in such a way of a claim and then does not take the opportunity of calling for documents, reports or witnesses prescribed in the club rules, can it then be presumed in such circumstances that the club has waived compliance with its rule of notification?

There are compelling reasons why the rule as to notification of a claim to the club by a member should be upheld. Although the club may hear of the claim by other means than directly from the member, it nevertheless remains important to know precisely how and when that claim will be presented. It is suggested that even where the club is aware of an event likely to give rise to a claim, the member remains bound to notify the club as soon as it becomes clear that the claim is to be pursued further. It is most certainly of extreme importance for the club to be informed when a member receives a writ or even more so when judgment is entered against him. Accordingly, the failure of a member to notify the club of significant events in the legal process of a claim deprives the club of its right to take over the conduct and control of the proceedings.

In this way the club is fully aware of all developments and is put in a position to exercise its rights to take control of the claim at what it considers to be the most appropriate time.

Together with the requirement for prompt notification of claims, clubs seek to protect themselves by laying down an absolute time-limit for the notification of potential claims.

Often this is combined with the provision requiring prompt notice.

The rules of some P & I associations are more strictly drafted and start the 12-month period running not from the time that the member has knowledge of any casualty, event or claim, but from the time which, in the opinion of the P & I club committee, the member ought to have known of any such occurrence. Although most clubs specify a prescription period of 12 months, some demand notification within only six months. In the case of clubs with a short prescription period the rules go on to provide that the assured will not forfeit his claim on the club if he can prove that it has been impossible for him to observe the time-limit and that he has advised his claim as soon as possible. Some club rules, however, also state that a member's claims for recovery shall nevertheless become time-barred 10 years after the damage occurred and the rules of some clubs imposing an absolute time bar may, if rigidly applied, lead to consequences unfair to members.

A number of these issues relating to club rules requiring notification were discussed by Mocatta, J in the case of *The 'Vainquer Jose'—CVG Siderurgicia del Orinoco SA* v. *London Steamship Mutual Assurance Association Ltd* (1979). This was a case of extreme importance to members of P & I associations.

In practice, of course, the usual procedure in the case of a casualty is that the master of the entered vessel would notify the nearest P & I club correspondents in the particular port or area and the club correspondents will in turn notify the club management and it is they in fact that quite often notify the member.

A MEMBER'S DUTY NOT TO ADMIT LIABILITY

It is generally expressed to be a condition precedent to a member's right of recovery from his club that no claim should be settled nor any liability admitted by or on behalf of the member without the prior consent of the club in writing. Most clubs generally provide in their rules that the acceptance of the member's claim under club cover is dependent on his liability being established by a judgment of a competent court or arbitration award or by an 'out of court' settlement which has been approved by the association.

The effect of these rules clearly illustrates the fact that it is not up to the member himself to admit his liability, such an admission of liability, of course, being binding on the club. The reason for these rules is that a member may be influenced to settle, for example, for purely business reasons by way of protecting a customer's interests in pursuit of his business.

The rules of some associations seek to give the member a much freer hand in settling minor claims without having to obtain the club's consent in advance. For example, a provision recognising such a possibility may state 'if . . . the assured has accepted the claim or paid compensation, the association does not cover the liability, unless the assured proves that the claim was justified both as regards basis and amount'.

Such an arrangement is of use particularly to members engaged in the liner trades, where the shipowner may provide his local agents with a 'settlement authority' which specifies a maximum amount, generally agreed in advance with the P & I club, for which the agent may settle claims. Under such an arrangement, when a voyage is regarded as terminated, as far as claims against the vessel are concerned, a general account together with invoices, debit notes and reasons for settling claims is normally to be sent to the club to obtain reimbursement. This situation does not, however, detract from the underlying principle behind the rule that the club cannot entertain claims settled for mere business purposes or reasons of goodwill, without any legal justification.

A MEMBER MUST HAVE BEEN FOUND LIABLE AND DISCHARGED THAT LIABILITY

The insurance coverage provided by P & I associations, termed quite frequently as 'liability' insurance, has in fact traditionally been one of 'indemnity'. Accordingly, an indemnity underwriter does not become committed to reimbursing an assured until the assured has actually paid the claim. Therefore, in the claims handling procedure once a claim has been settled and agreed it is for the member to pay the settlement funds to discharge the claim in the first instance before seeking reimbursement from the P & I association.

The distinction made between an indemnity and liability policy is that payment by the assured is necessary under an indemnity insurance before the insurer is involved, whereas this is not required under liability insurance. Today, in this latter form of insurance the underwriter comes on risk as soon as the assured becomes liable.

P & I associations undertake only to pay the amount which the member shall have become liable to pay and shall have paid. And a proviso often admits that there is a possibility of the member or the claims handling department of the club's managers making a 'good deal' in an out of court settlement. Settlements out of court are usually offered on the basis, albeit without prejudice, that the decision of the court would have been detrimental to the defendant. Another exception to this general principle is the occasion when the club has given a cargo-owner a guarantee against damage to cargo carried in an entered vessel and the cargo-owner demands payment under that club guarantee. This would come within the principle that any decision of a court could be predicted as being against the member. The most common situation where the club will waive strict compliance with this condition precedent is where it has, at an early stage, taken control of the handling of the claim and settles directly with the claimant. However, the mere fact that the club has taken over the handling of the claim is not to be taken as an admission of the club's liability to pay the claim and the club always has discretion as to whether to waive compliance with this rule.

CLUB LETTERS OF UNDERTAKING

One of the most important and popular facilities afforded by P & I associations is their assistance in securing the release of vessels that have been arrested in a variety of circumstances. Although normally no reference will be found in the rules of the associations with regard to this important facility, the clubs do provide on behalf of their members guarantees or letters of undertaking in order that an entered ship may be released from arrest or indeed from the threat of arrest.

Club letters of undertaking have increasingly gained respectability and acceptance in parts of the world where formerly only bank guarantees were accepted. Most claimants are prepared to accept a club letter of undertaking, which of course is a great convenience as it avoids substantial delays.

Although the possibility of releasing property under arrest by methods other than the provision of bail or payment into court is recognised in the rules of the Supreme Court, the club letter of undertaking is now the most usual form of release and it would appear that in the United Kingdom an arresting party is still entitled to insist on bail or payment into court before consenting to release.

It is difficult to see why a club letter of undertaking should not be acceptable as a 'sufficient security' unless the financial standing of the club or its bona fides is successfully challenged. The amount of security specified in the club letter of undertaking is usually the limitation figure or the value of the *res* or, in the event of a dispute as to the amount of security, the figure determined by the court.

In the main, most of the P & I associations have a standard letter of undertaking which provides that in consideration of the claimant releasing from arrest and/or refraining from arresting the particular vessel, which may be the entered vessel or any other ship in the same ownership, associated ownership or management as the particular vessel, the club will undertake to pay to the claimant's solicitors on his behalf, on demand, such sums as may be awarded to the claimant in proceedings before a court of competent jurisdiction or in arbitration proceedings in a particular venue, up to a specified maximum amount. The said undertaking often states that the club undertakes, within a specified period of time from the receipt of a request to do so, to accept on behalf of the shipowner service of proceedings and to acknowledge service, without prejudice to the application, which may be made to the court or a stay of such proceedings or for the release of the security.

Another form of guarantee often provided by the clubs is a so-called 'cargo receiver's indemnity'. This occurs in circumstances where a vessel arrives with damaged cargo and the receiver refuses delivery of most or all of the cargo. This leaves the carrier to rely upon the local court to determine whether the cargo receiver has such a right of refusal or the carrier has a duty to dispose of the cargo himself. In practice, however, the cargo receiver would take delivery provided he has secured his claim against the carrier by obtaining a suitable guarantee. Where the carrier's club is satisfied that the cargo claim will fall within the ambit of the club cover then the club may provide a letter of undertaking which will always seek to preserve the defences that are open to the carrier under the contract of carriage, together with the appropriate rights of limitation and the proper law and forum provided for in the contract of carriage. The clubs will provide letters of undertaking, where acceptable, to release vessels detained for reasons such as customs penalties and other state fines, but in some countries clearance is refused until a fine is paid.

Although clubs provide a very valuable service to their members and are indeed in a unique position to help those members who have found themselves in difficult circumstances, this service related to the provision of letters of undertaking is not available on demand.

The clubs have adopted certain rules in order to safeguard themselves from having this facility abused and club literature is very careful in its drafting to make it clear that letters of undertaking and guarantees are provided only in appropriate cases.

The putting up of security, therefore, is a matter purely at the club's discretion and has been described as a mere 'act of friendship' on the part of a club. The clubs have never been willing to accept the provision of bail or security as a duty under their standard form of cover.

The vessel which the member wishes to have released must be entered in the association at the time of the casualty giving rise to the claim or it must be a vessel which is in the same ownership, associated ownership or management as the vessel responsible for the claim.

The service of providing security is usually extended only to owner members and not time charterer members. Where a chartered vessel is arrested it is a general rule that the owner's club and not the charterer's club arranges security provided that there is no prejudice suffered through the internal division of liability of the charter-party between the parties themselves.

Another aspect of utmost importance is to assess whether the risk which has given rise to the claim itself is indeed covered under the particular member's terms of entry with the P & I associations. For instance, if the claim itself fell below the applicable deductible or is indeed specifically excluded from the cover, a guarantee from the club may not be available.

In addition to being part of the club's cover, the incident in respect of which the vessel has been arrested must give rise to a true liability against the member. Clubs do not under any circumstances give unconditional guarantees, such guarantees are always conditional on the liability of the member being agreed between the parties or established by a competent court.

DIRECT ACTION

No book on P & I insurance would be complete without comment being made upon the ability under English law of third-party claimants to take legal action direct against insurers when their claim in its original form was against the assured (or in the case of the clubs) a club member.

The statute relevant to such procedure is the Third Parties (Rights Against Insurers) Act 1930 which was originally introduced to give relief to the increasing number of innocent people who suffered at the hands of the fast-growing band of motorists who in those days had a habit of going bankrupt at the wrong moment.

The preamble to the Act, which explains its reason for existence, states that it is 'an Act to confer on third parties rights against insurers of third-party risks in the event of the assured becoming insolvent and in certain other events'. The two most important provisions of the Act are contained in section 1(1) and (3). The gist of the first is that if the insured becomes bankrupt or has made some sort of arrangement with his creditors or, if he is a company, then in the event of a winding-up order being made or a resolution for a voluntary winding-up being passed, etc., in respect of any liability being incurred by the insured his rights against the insurer under the contract of insurance in respect of the liability shall, notwithstanding anything in any Act or rule of law to the contrary, be transferred to and vested in the third party to whom the liability was so incurred.

The other subsection provides that any contract of insurance which purports either directly or indirectly to avoid a contract of insurance, or to alter the rights of the parties in the case that any of the events mentioned in the earlier subsection arise, the contract shall have no effect, assuming, of course, that the particular contract was entered into after the coming into effect of the Act.

The principal implication of these various provisions is that the statute does not confer direct rights on the third party against the insurer. It does not literally transfer the claim itself to the third party but merely has the effect of transferring those rights which the insured person or company has or had against his insurer (the club) under the relevant contracts of insurance (or, in club parlance, under the club's rules). To put it another way what the third party is actually doing in the event that he successfully takes action under the 1930 statute, is 'stepping into the shoes of the insured person or company'. If he wishes to succeed, the third party must establish various points:

(a) That there is in existence an effective contract of insurance between the insured who has incurred a liability to him and the insurer.
(b) That the particular liability which has been incurred is covered by the relevant contract of insurance.
(c) That the insured person or company has been made bankrupt or closed in liquidation or put in a similar position by some sort of court order as contemplated by section 1 of the Act.
(d) That the rights of the insured against his insurer can effectively be transferred.
(e) That he, the third party, can successfully counter any defences which the insurer might put up against him under the terms and conditions of the insurance contract (or in the case of the clubs, the rules of the club).

P & I clubs have become involved in direct action cases on several occasions in this and the last decade and it would perhaps be as good a method as any of illustrating the problem to list and comment upon these cases.

In *In Re Compagnia Merabello San Nicolas SA* (1973), a P & I club made a bid to oppose an application by a third-party judgment creditor to wind up the shipowning (member) company for no other reason than that the owner member owed calls to the club. The court decided that this was an insufficient reason and that all that the third party need show, as it could on the facts in that case, was that it had a viable claim of a P & I type with reasonable chances of succeeding.

In Re Allobrogia Steamship Corporation (1979) was a parallel case. This case and the *Merabello* case were heard in the companies court as the matter at issue was an attempt to block a winding-up order.

Cases subsequent to those two, of which the most highly publicised was *The 'Vainqueur Jose'*, were brought before the commercial court since the issue there was the ability of a club to defend itself against a third party's claim direct. In *The 'Vainqueur Jose'* (1971), by the time the matter reached the commercial court a winding-up order had been obtained from London's companies court leaving a path clear for the third party (who was a Puerto Rico-based cargo claimant) to proceed direct against the wound-up owner's P & I club. The claim was in two parts—one for forwarding charges which had been incurred on the cargo after the ship had broken down at an intermediate port on the contractual route and the other for damages. The P & I club was not seeking to show that, as a mutual insurance association, they were immune from suit. That basic point had been settled years previously. The clubs *are* insurers (like any market insurer) within the meaning of the 1930 Act. The London club's defence was that the member himself had, whilst he was still in existence, exhibited conduct at the time of or subsequent to the happening of the casualty to the ship, which had he himself advanced the claim, would have entitled the committee of the club to reject or reduce his claim. The conduct referred to was a failure to notify the club of the incident which gave rise to a claim within the time stipulated in the rules (one year) and a failure to act as a prudent uninsured—i.e. to take legal action in order to limit his liability. His failure to notify the club deprived the club of the chance to take action on his behalf to limit liability. Forwarding charges are excluded from club cover unless at the discretion of the committee they are admitted. The court recognised that the structure of P & I insurance was such that many of the recoveries to be made by members of the club were only at the discretion of the club's committee. It recognised the degree of control and the extent of the power of rejection or reduction which the committee had over a member's claim. The discretionary power is most clearly illustrated in the operation of the 'omnibus rule', that popular (from the member's point of view) provision which allows for a whole miscellany of claims to be given consideration which do not otherwise fit into any specified risk/rule but are deserving of a chance to be included under a member's club cover. But the court has to satisfy itself that the discretion which the committee is granted under the rules is exercised in good faith since, if it was not, the club could not use it as a shield to defend itself against third-party claims brought direct. In *The 'Vainqueur Jose'*, the court obviously did satisfy itself on this point since the club won the case.

So, by the commencement of the 1980s the interpretation of the 1930 Act had reached the point where the clubs were powerless to obstruct the winding up of the members but they could mount a successful defence on the rules on the same lines as they would have rejected or reduced the same claim had it been presented to the club by the member himself.

This was, however, by no means the total absolution of the matter. More law suits emerged. In 1984 a P & I club was defendant to *Socony Mobil (The 'Padre Island')* the issue in that case being whether the club could hold the third party (Mobil) to the arbitration clause in the club's rules under which all disputes between members and the club should be referred to arbitration and only after an award could the matter be taken by either party to court for review. The so-called *Scott* v. *Avery* provision (which forms the concluding part of the arbitration clause) was also under review. This standard provision reads as follows: 'no member may bring or maintain any action, suit or other legal proceedings against the association in connection with any such difference or dispute unless he has first obtained an arbitration award in accordance with the rules'.

The High Court judge (Leggatt, J) held that the third party was limited only to whatever cause of action he was entitled to under the Act and that the Act transferred to him only those contractual rights which the now wound-up insured had. These included the arbitration clause. As the dispute had not at that stage been taken to arbitration, the High Court action was stayed in favour of arbitration. Mobil then proceeded to arbitration, their argument being that the club could 'pay up' their cargo claim as the shipowner member had been wound up within the jurisdiction as allowed under the 1930 Act and all its rights against the club had vested in Mobil, the unpaid third-party claimant. The arbitrator disagreed. He had in mind the club's Rule 2, by which the club's promise to indemnify a member was conditional upon a member not only incurring a liability but having actually paid the claim (this emphasises the clear distinction between a liability underwriter and an indemnity underwriter). The award having been made, Mobil was free under the *Scott* v. *Avery* provision to go to the High Court on appeal, just prior to that, however, yet another High Court decision had been handed down (*The 'Fanti'*) which ruled that an owner of cargo with an outstanding claim against the carrying vessel owner whom the claimant had wound up because of his inability to pay could claim from the P & I club under the indemnity agreement.

The 'Fanti' had come at an inopportune time, right between the arbitration award on *The 'Padre Island'* and Mobil's appeal on that award. Counsel for Mobil naturally relied on it and pressed the argument that the effect of section 1 of the 1930 Act was to transfer to the third-party creditor both the rights obtained under club cover and also the terms of the contract—in practical terms the club's rules. But amongst these rules is the 'pay first' rule which obliges the member to pay the claim first as a condition precedent to claiming recovery from the club less any deductible which may be applicable. *The 'Fanti'* judge had said that to transfer that particular rule would be absurd and futile and that it should be disregarded. *The 'Padre Island'* judge disagreed with him and thus a conflict resulted between two High Court judges on whether a club member's right to be indemnified could be inherited by a third-party claimant. What rights, asked *The 'Padre Island'* judge, did the owner have against the club at the material time, i.e. at the time of the winding-up? He had no *present* right of indemnity. If he had no present right of indemnity then this right could not be transferred to the third party. To merely ignore it as 'futile' was not the correct approach. It is not possible to ignore such a basic term. The inescapable fact was that it was a term that was unfulfilled at the time of the transfer of rights to Mobil and thus as there was no right to indemnity then there was no right passed. Mobil's other argument was that section 1(3) of the Act made of no effect any contract of insurance which purported to take away the rights of third parties. Counsel for the club countered this by remarking that club rules generally speaking were drafted and used long before the 1930 Act. The judge rejected Mobil's contentions by saying that there was nothing in the Act to support 'such a startling and wide-ranging inroad' into the parties' freedom to contract on what terms they chose.

So developments in case law in the field of direct action against the club seem to have reached a point where it is not certain whether this club rule will be upheld. The discretionary power of the committee seems well recognised providing it is exercised bona fides. The 'pay first' rule, from being ignored and treated as futile, may be one which alone can block a third party's practical ability to claim direct from the concerned club simply because a right which does not exist, because a condition precedent has not been fulfilled, cannot be transferred to and inherited by the third party.

6

P & I CLUB REINSURANCE AND THE INTERNATIONAL GROUP

REINSURANCE

A club could not exist on its own in modern conditions. Liabilities which shipowners and other maritime people face are or can be catastrophic and one has merely to point to the *Amoco Cadiz* and the *Torrey Canyon* for examples. Thus a club needs reinsurance—the security which enables it with a clear conscience and peace of mind to offer its members unlimited cover, and perhaps even more importantly the assurance that claims, however gigantic in value, will be paid promptly. This latter benefit provided by the clubs to their members is possibly one of the most attractive to them.

Under the mutual system, the club has the power to call upon its members to supplement the funds originally levied by further contributions up to, in theory, an unlimited extent. Indeed, this was the way in which clubs met their liabilities before the invention and advent of reinsurance as we now know it. But 'passing the hat round' the membership to meet catastrophe type claims proved the death of some of the early mutuals when members foundered financially in the face of unexpectedly high supplementary calls.

How is reinsurance achieved and at the same time the overall cost of insurance kept down to a level where the clubs can still boast insurance at the minimum cost? Answer: by doing it mutually. The clubs themselves associate together in order to reinsure each other on a mutual basis—(and here is mutuality at its height) in excess of a retained amount of US$1,200,000, any one claim. This mutual commitment of the clubs for the benefit of each other's membership is crystallised in what is known as the pooling agreement. It is largely based on trust and confidence from which springs the holding club's ability to pay a claim far in excess of the retention and know that the excess balance will be forthcoming without any embarrassing and constant reminders and without the need of the other paying clubs to get prior approval of the holding club's claim settlement figure. Indeed, the pooling agreement could not operate other than at an extremely high level of mutual trust and confidence and if ever rate cutting became rife to the point of a rate war between the group clubs, then the pooling agreement would inevitably cease to exist effectively.

However, unlimited cover is not achieved by the pooling agreement alone because that has a ceiling limit upon it for any one claim of US$12,000,000. Beyond that figure, additional reinsurance is obtained on the open market with reinsurers of high quality, led by Lloyd's, with a combined purchasing power generated by approximately 93% of the world's tonnage (entered in one or other of the group clubs)—said to be the largest reinsurance contract in the world, it was first introduced in 1951. But even this market reinsurance has limits—presently standing at US$1.25 billion. By some ironical twist, the clubs, who have consistently advertised their services as being a 'better alternative' than the market, are obliged to look to that same 'market' for the higher echelons of their reinsurance programme.

If a claim were to exceed this mammoth figure, the excess reverts back to the pool to be shared amongst the members of the pooling agreement. In that event each club would pay its share in proportion to its entered tonnage and not its call income. Provision is made for this eventuality by some of the clubs who maintain a 'catastrophe' fund which could be used to finance a 'catastrophe call'.

This substantially 'keep it in the family' reinsurance programme ensures not only minimum cost of maximum (in fact unlimited) cover but also stability of costs over the long term. If the ultimate aim of club managers is to offer their members unlimited cover then this sophisticated arrangement probably could not be bettered as a way of enabling them to do so. During this decade, however, there have been dissenting voices in the International Group who have argued for placing a limit on cover. But in these days of high values or values steadily increasing it is far from unthinkable for there to arise a claim valued at US$2 billion involving a liquid gas carrier in a built-up area or a massive incident in a highly populated area ruled by a particularly sensitive government, a sort of '*Torrey Canyon* dressed up in 1987 rig'. Bearing in mind that US$2 billion is exactly US$1 billion over the maximum limit for the year 1987 to 1988, there would be a fat balance having to be borne by the overspill arrangements. There is no general 'overspill' insurance so that each club must make its own provision for the funding of overspill claims. The alternatives are that a club would either:

1. set aside reserves earmarked for payment of pay overspill claims; or
2. take out a stop loss policy (see below for explanation); or
3. purchase special catastrophe reinsurance up to whatever limit they can obtain.

Whichever alternative is chosen there will be a limit (overall) set somewhere. So there is a very real fear of a need arising to levy further calls. Clearly an increase in the reinsurance contract ceiling limit will not keep pace with the corresponding increase in the values of catastrophe claims.

Reinsurance under the pooling system has two objectives, one to provide club members with unlimited cover at minimal cost and the second to provide the greatest security possible for the membership as a whole. What would happen if, for example, the 'pool' system disintegrated? One immediate reaction would be that the high level of mutual trust and confidence which exists between the Group clubs, and upon which is founded the practice of paying claims promptly and on demand and without the prior need to be reimbursed by the reinsuring clubs, would vanish. This is perhaps one of the greatest bargaining points which the clubs have over market insurers when it comes to attracting members/assureds to their fold—the prompt payment of claims. Another inevitable consequence would be that the costs of reinsurance would jump so that no club could cope with the massive extra risks on its own, they would each individually need to seek reinsurance on the market which could cost more and would involve additional brokerage. Above all the benefits of unlimited cover would disappear for good.

The pooling arrangement exhibits clear advantages. First,

because of the lack of any profit element in the P & I system the 'first layer' of reinsurance is virtually free of charge to the assureds. No panic at all and no cost is felt until the loss is actually paid out under the pooling agreement. Secondly, because of the huge worldwide spread of tonnage entered in the group clubs overall, one claim, or the effect of it, is spread and thus cushioned throughout this vast fleet of insured ships. So, the premium for the second layer, the excess loss contract with Lloyd's, is brought to the very lowest level. It is the very international flavour of the clubs which provides this strength and it is the lack of ability to acquire a widely diversified portfolio which is the main obstacle to the establishment by developing countries of national or regional P & I clubs. With approximately 90% of the world's 400 million gross registered tonnage of oceangoing vessels entered in the clubs of the International Group, one claim can be spread throughout almost the whole tonnage of the world. The size of the International Group and the spread of risks is such that the excess reinsurance premium is more favourable than any individual owner could purchase on his own. A P & I club, like any other insurer, must diversify its portfolio as much as possible. This is achieved with the clubs themselves striving, through the group system, for the widest possible geographical spread of membership. The Group operates as if it was one huge mutual club with a massive spread of risk and widely diversified portfolio.

The sharing of claims between the major P & I clubs has led inevitably to a wide sharing of experience of different types of claim and often the clubs of the group will act jointly. One of the consequences of this reinsurance arrangement is that the risks that are covered by the club should be very similar and club rules must be consistent. In fact, regular discussions between managers of clubs in the pool are held in order to agree on policy decisions regarding new risks or amendments to existing cover. Decisions taken by the group managers are then referred to the committees or boards of directors of the pool clubs for consideration and ratification.

Club rules and the scope of the club cover should not only be similar in character but should also receive similar or consistent interpretation by the clubs of the International

Group. Too flexible an approach towards the enforcement of its rules or the application of its cover by one club may admit a claim to be settled which other clubs of the group would not have contemplated as within the limits of P & I insurance. In the case of a large claim, requiring the involvement of the market insurance arrangements, the reinsurers could even refuse to reimburse an over-generous club.

THE INTERNATIONAL GROUP

The clubs who are party to the pooling agreement have formed themselves into what is known as the 'International Group'. They number 17 in all. Of these only two are *not* members of the pooling agreement. Originally, when the pool system was first introduced in 1899, the group was merely the London Group and the original clubs were: Britannia, London, North of England, Sunderland, Standard, UK, Newcastle, West of England and Steamship Mutual. Added to those to form the current international group are: Liverpool and London, Swedish, Skuld, Gard, Japan and Shipowners' Mutual. The non-UK based clubs have over the years made interim arrangements for reinsurance by 'pairing up' with a Group club, e.g. Japan Club with Britannia, Skuld with the London Club, and by 'hitching a lift' in this way they became indirect members of the pool. In practice, club A (the reinsured club) had its own retention for each claim and also the retention for club B (the reinsuring club). By dint of this 'piggy back' system the small (in the old days) non-UK based club could gain access not only to the pool but also to the benefits of the group excess loss contract and thus circumvent the fiercely nationalistic policies regarding reinsurance whereby they might be required to place all their reinsurance cover on the local market no matter what the cost. Scandinavian clubs joined the group as full members in 1981. From the foregoing it is clear that the clubs' retentions both individually and as a group are respectively kept at a high level leaving only really the catastrophic element in any one claim to be covered by market insurance. Entry of a club to the group is not simple. The likelihood is that any club less than five years old will be refused admission and in any event would be unlikely to have the degree of financial stability and 'respectability' which the group would demand.

Further functions of the International Group are (a) to act as a representative body representing over 90% of the world's tonnage; and (b) to offer a voice against governments or non-governmental organisations. In 1981 the group was incorporated as a company and thus could effectively act in the role of observer at functions on an international level.

STOP LOSS POLICIES

One method whereby a club can stabilise its costs and thus assume in outward appearances the security which members, and particularly their brokers, like to see, is to take out what is known as a 'stop loss' policy. The effect of such a policy is to put a 'brake' on the level of supplementary calls levied by the club to replenish a shortfall in funds to pay claims in any one particular policy year. For example, if a policy is taken out covering an excess beyond an estimated 30% call, then if a 50% call is found to be warranted by the club's underwriters, the policy picks up that excess, subject to whatever limit the policy may have upon it. The stop loss policy is an alternative method for a club to cover itself against the requirement for 'overspill' funds where no special provisions for catastrophic calls are made in the club rules and supplementary calls to cater for the excess which is over the upper limit of the excess policy are required.

As well as protecting the top end of the scale, clubs, especially small ones, have been keen in recent years to protect their retentions by taking out stop loss policies. This may be more a political than an economic move, though whatever it is, it is certain that high in the priorities of club management philosophy is stability of costs and effective hedging against violent swings in the pendulum of supplementary calls.

Underwriters of stop loss policies have a tough job because the risk, which in reality they are being asked to assume, is that of the shrewdness, or lack of it, of underwriting expertise, an indefinable question mark, if ever there was one.

THE INTERNATIONAL GROUP AGREEMENT

For the International Group to operate it is necessary for the member clubs to behave in a responsible manner towards each other when competing for business. If clubs within the group were to engage in rate cutting this could result in a lack of stability amongst the clubs and therefore a lack of stability in the International Group. In order to prevent unreasonable competition among the clubs the members of the International Group have entered into an agreement known as 'the International Group Agreement' (IGA).

The precise terms of the IGA are detailed and complex and beyond the scope of this work, but may be summarised as follows. First, the IGA operates only in the case of new entries and seeks to ensure that a ship entered with its existing club will not be quoted unreasonably low call rates should it wish to change to a new club. Secondly, where a new vessel is about to become part of a fleet then if the whole fleet is insured in one club then any other club should not offer unreasonably low call rates in respect of this new vessel. The IGA provides for a committee for the purposes of hearing references under the agreement.

The IGA appeared to work well between the clubs but recently attracted the attention of the European Commission as *prima facie* contravening EEC regulations relating to free competition. The EEC Commission took the view that shipowners ought to be able to obtain free quotes on vessels and that the IGA provided a restriction upon this right. In July 1984, the Commission sent to the International Group a statement of objections which were grounds for finding that parts of the IGA infringed the Treaty of Rome. In response to this the group submitted an amended IGA known as the 'Modified IGA 1984' which the EEC has decided would be acceptable until 20 February 1995, at which time it will be reviewed.

7

SPECIALIST CLUBS

DEFENCE ASSOCIATIONS

The title 'defence associations' is misleading because the implication is that the assistance given by the club to its members who have this class of cover is only in respect of defending claims, but the fact is that assistance is given as much in prosecuting claims as defending. What is even less intelligible is the expression 'FD & D' which stands for freight, demurrage and defence, which even more blatantly appears to exclude the process of prosecution of claims. Freight and demurrage, or rather claims in respect of those two payments, are merely two of a myriad of disputes which can potentially arise from a charter-party agreement.

What would seem to be a more explanatory title for this class of cover is 'legal cost' cover, for what must be clearly understood in this class of cover is that the sum in dispute is *not* insured. There are probably many who believe, probably because they have been misled by the title—freight, demurrage and defence—that the sums of e.g. demurrage or freight are actually insured and that the club is not only on risk for the award, if adverse to the member, but also for the costs incurred in achieving it or failing to achieve it as the case may be. Nothing could be further from the truth. If demurrage, or more accurately the risk of not being able to recover demurrage, is insurable, it is not so in the clubs, but only in the proprietary marine market. Indeed P & I cover as we have seen elsewhere in this book specifically *excludes* demurrage, or as the rules put it rather more comprehensively—freight, demurrage, hire or detention. Loss of hire can be insured in a special club catering exclusively for that risk.

What does the 'defence' class cover? A loose definition

would be anything not covered by the P & I class, but this is a little too dangerous to take at its face value. Certainly, a proviso to defence cover is that 'no member shall be entitled to receive in this class any amount which would be recoverable under the insurances aforesaid or which he is or would be entitled, but for his entry in this class, to recover under any other insurance or otherwise howsoever'. Generally speaking, the disputes which are covered by FD & D are charter-party disputes of which freight, demurrage or deadfreight are common examples. But bearing in mind that FD & D and P & I are mutually exclusive, there are charter-party disputes which would not come under FD & D but would fall under P & I. An example of this is cargo damage which has occurred on a vessel which at the material time was time chartered. Where the actual owners are faced with a damage claim from the bill of lading holder and since, under English law, the owners are deemed to be the carriers, they negotiate the claim but seek under the charter-party to be reimbursed by the charterers who under the charter-party terms are usually made responsible. Although that secondary indemnity action by owner against charterer is technically a charter-party dispute, it falls to be handled under P & I cover because being cargo *damage* it is merely an extension (by way of further indemnity action) to a cargo damage claim.

In addition to coverage of charter-party disputes, other contracts into which a shipowner/member might enter are covered. Examples of such being sale and purchase contracts, stevedoring contracts, contracts of insurance on hull, cargo or freight or mortgage agreements. Some clubs sum up this extension of the cover under the subheading 'breach of any charter-party, bill of lading *or other contract*'. This phrase exposes itself to the question: do not bill of lading disputes overspill into P & I? For example, cargo loss or damage could be described as resulting from a breach of bill of lading obligations and should properly fall to be dealt with under the cargo rule in P & I. This is true, but then the general rule applies that what falls under P & I cannot be dealt with under FD & D, so that FD & D is concerned with only those matters that *no* other insurance picks up.

The consultancy service given by the clubs' managers does

not or should not confine itself to the period *after* a dispute has arisen, though that clearly is a substantial part of it. Club managers hold themselves ready to advise on problems unconnected with a particular dispute, e.g. the drafting or amending of charter-party clause, the redesigning of the terms and conditions of the bill of lading. The club managers are 'the friendly shoulder to cry on'—they are, or should be, good listeners as well as good advisers.

Clearly there can be claims which would appear, if viewed solely within their own context, to be 'straight' FD & D, but if examined more closely are extensions of P & I claims. Take as a hypothetical example an injury to a US longshoreman on board a ship which at the time was under time charter on, say, a New York Produce Exchange Form. The claim for personal injury damage brought (presumably, though not necessarily) against the shipowners would be a P & I claim and fall to be handled by the owner's P & I club. But if after settlement (or payment of the court award) by the owners with their club's approval, those owners, with their club's support, choose to seek recovery from the charterer under the terms of the charter-party (implied indemnity provisions), this would not be a fresh dispute falling within the ambit of FD & D charter-party legal cost cover, but would remain within the scope of the personal injury rule under the P & I class of cover. And from the point of view of the charterer defending against this indemnity claim, he too would need to call upon his liability insurers. They could be one of the shipowners' clubs who do take a few charterer members or the exclusively charterers' club or a market insurer.

It is misleading to define FD & D cover as 'anything outside P & I'. A defence association will expect that its members have taken out adequate insurance in other traditional areas, i.e. particularly hull and machinery and war risks. Thus, if there is a hull damage claim for which the ship's owners are minded to dispute with some other party, e.g. a stevedore or a charterer (but not, of course, a collision claim which *is* a P & I matter), then primarily the hull underwriter is the interested underwriter. However, there may be a large (or small) deductible in the hull policy obliging the assured owner to bear so much of the claim (on the policy) for his own account. That amount may exceed the claimed amount if the damage was minor.

To illustrate the benefits which can be gained from membership of a defence club a topical law suit, which has just passed through the final appeal stage (House of Lords), involves the vessel *The 'Kysikos'*. The relevant charter-party contained 'wibon' provisions which purported to allow the master to tender his notice of readiness whether or not he had reached his berth, provided that in all other relevant respects he is ready and able to work cargo. The dispute was over who pays for waiting time or, in other words, does the charterer owe the owner demurrage in this case worth $30,000? The arbitrator said that the effect of putting in wibon is to convert a berth charter into a port charter, which in turn has the effect of advancing the commencement of laytime to start earlier whatever it may be which prevents the ship from berthing. The High Court disagreed. The judge found for owners.

This dispute is clearly one which is of interest to a wide section of the shipping community, both owners and charterers, and is not a 'one-off' disagreement between merely two parties. Thus the taking of this particular dispute to the final court of appeal (the House of Lords) and the obtaining of a successful result by the charterers should be a great legal advantage to the voyage chartering community generally.

However, a small or average size charterer might well be unable to fund such an appeal out of his own coffers since the costs of an appeal of this sort to the top court in the land may well exceed the amount of money in dispute. If, however, a shipowner or charterer has an entry in a defence club then provided that the directors of that club have approved the taking of the particular piece of legal action and have indicated their support for a member in pursuing a dispute through a particular piece of litigation or arbitration, then the costs of so doing are paid out of club funds—subject to any deductible amount (say 25%) which the member may have agreed to bear from his own account.

The cover provided by defence clubs, or by the defence class of P & I clubs, is, it may be said, of a more discretionary nature than is the P & I cover. The discretion reveals itself in two main ways. First, discretion as to whether the club will support a member in fighting a particular claim (or in defending it) through the courts or, more likely, because of the very common insertion of arbitration agreements in the charter-parties, before an arbitration tribunal. The club preserves the right to take over conduct of the case and to decide in its absolute discretion (through committee decision) whether to support contesting of the case. As an additional discretionary point, the committee is empowered to authorise the payment out of club funds of the amount in dispute if it is satisfied that the amount of legal money which would be needed to fully pursue the claim or to defend it to the full would exceed that sum. This underlines the attitude of the clubs generally that the decision to fight cases should not rest on a matter of principle alone, but on the economics of a particular case, unless, of course, the principle to be tested is of wide interest to a large section of the membership.

A second, smaller matter for the exercise of discretion is as to how wide the definition of legal costs/expenses/disbursements should be stretched. Should it be confined strictly to the *legal* costs? Or should the costs of other services used to further the success of a particular claim be included within defence cover? For instance, the survey costs of examining a bunker sample where the allegation has been that a charterer has breached his charter-party commitments to provide bunkers of suitable quality. On this latter point it would be wrong to make any attempt at a general answer since each club pursues its own policy and each individual claim or case has its own individual circumstances which might make it reasonable or unreasonable to accept such expenses for club account.

STRIKE CLUBS

Cover in respect of strikes is another non-P & I form of insurance which has become available to shipowners and charterers on a mutual basis. In London, strike associations have existed since about 1947 when the Shipowner's Mutual Strike Insurance Association was formed. Soon after that it became the practice for the managers of the major P & I associations to establish a strike class within their clubs. A leader now in this specialist field is Transmarine Mutual.

Insurance against strikes is relatively simple when compared with the comparatively complicated rules of an average P & I association. P & I risks, as has been seen earlier in this book, are legion compared with the simple idea of whether or not a ship has been delayed by a strike and its owners have suffered a loss as a result of that delay. Perhaps as good a definition as any of what is a 'strike', is 'any form of industrial action taken by workers which is carried out with the intention of preventing, restricting or otherwise interfering with the production of goods or the provision of services'.

As with war risks so with strike risks there are areas in the world which are considered to be 'bad risks' and an obvious example of this is Australia where the instances of dock strikes are more common than possibly any other country in the world. Perhaps an equally citable example would be Spain. Because there are countries which have acquired a bad reputation for waterfront strikes there is a tendency for an owner to attempt to cover himself by strike insurance when he knows he is facing a strike situation. A strike club would be unable to accept him for membership or, if he was already a member, would be unlikely to reimburse him by way of recovery if he was sending his ship into a known strike situation. This is on the same principle that one cannot purchase insurance in respect of fire when you notice that your house is beginning to smoulder.

The risks covered by a strike club are set out in three parts which are (1) direct delay, (2) indirect delay and (3) crew strikes. Direct delay, as the expression implies, is delay caused directly by a strike and is thus limited to that period during which the strike is in progress. Indirect delay relates to that period after the strike has terminated but the vessel is still delayed due, for example, to congestion caused directly as a result of the strike. Crew strikes cover delay to an entered ship directly resulting from a strike of its own officers or crew.

The deductible applicable to this type of insurance is not a sum of money as in the case of P & I cover, where each risk tends to carry a different financial deductible and also the requirements of the member are relevant as to how much of the claim he is prepared to bear for his own account. With strikes risk insurance the deductible is reckoned in numbers of days, and as to how long the deductible period is, depends upon the area to which the vessel is trading and the susceptibility of that particular area to strikes either of short or long duration. To take Australia as the worst example, strike clubs would have to insist on a high deductible whereas trading to countries such as Italy or France where strikes are intermittent, possibly even occur regularly, but are not each of great duration and causative of massive delays, would call for a lower deductible.

A simple but typical calculation of a strike claim might be as follows. A vessel owner has requested to be covered for a 12-month period and has agreed an entered daily sum of £5,000 and has taken the maximum cover of 30 days with a deductible of four days. For worldwide trading the owner is likely to be charged as a premium about two days of EDS (i.e. the daily running cost) meaning an annual premium of £10,000. Supposing his ship is delayed by a strike for more than 30 days, he would recover from the club 30 times £5,000 = £150,000 less four times £5,000 (deductible) − £20,000 = £130,000.

To take another simple illustration, if the delay to the ship extends beyond the termination of the strike due to the consequences of the strike (e.g. causing port congestion) the owner could recover from the club for the whole period. Thus a strike which itself lasts 12 days on top of which there is a four-day delay due to the consequences resulting in a total of 16 days delay = £80,000 bulk claim, less deductible four times £5,000 leaves a net claim of £60,000.

The spirit of the mutual strike club is similar to that of a mutual P & I club, that is to say that the club exists for its members, indeed the club *is* its members. Therefore, where a member takes action to avoid the immediate effects of a strike which results in a loss to him of a different kind to the normal loss claim from a strike club, which is loss of days in delay, e.g. when a strike has commenced during loading and the owner (after consulting his club) sails without completing loading and finishes up with a net loss of freight income which is a smaller sum than that which would have been his loss of time claim on the club if he had ridden out the strike, his smaller claim would almost certainly be acceptable to the strike club's directors.

Arguably the incidence of strikes hits a shipowner's cash flow harder than any other occurrence covered by any other form of mutual insurance. Thus the claims staff of a strike club have a specially deep commitment to settle claims, if not immediately, in the minimum time.

LOSS OF HIRE OR EARNINGS

Clubs specialising in this risk are few, in fact there is only one currently in existence in London, Transmarine Mutual. It is designed to assist shipowners who are deprived of their ships' earning capacity as a result of breakdown of machinery or of certain perils listed in the institute time clauses (hulls) or the equivalent Norwegian or American forms. A certain number of days is agreed by each member with the managers, when he enters his ships and recoverable claims are limited to the period which is in excess of that agreed number of days. No member may recover more than 180 times his entered daily rate as recorded in the certificate of entry in respect of each policy year or agreed period of entry. The entered daily rate is a sum agreed with the club's managers and is based on the estimated daily earnings of the ship whilst it is engaged on the particular trade which the member should disclose and warrant in the application form when he applies to enter the vessel in the club. There can be no recovery from the club in the event that the breakdown which results in the loss of earning capacity is the sole and only result of wear and tear or of a lack of due diligence by the member himself.

There are those who argue, rightly or wrongly, that this type of risk is not suited to the mutual concept and should be covered, if at all, on the market at fixed premiums. The supporting argument for this view is that the nature of the risk does not require the claims handling expertise and legal consultancy service which the clubs traditionally provide, and which are strong factors amongst the general benefits of mutual club membership. In P & I insurance there is a 'common enemy'—the third party. In loss of hire insurance there is no common enemy. A member merely proves his claim against the club for recovery. The continued popularity of Transmarine Mutual demonstrates defiance of these arguments.

CHARTERERS' CLUBS

We will have seen that in the year 1854 the first shipowners' protection association was formed. One hundred and thirty-two years later, in the year 1986, the first ever charterers' mutual assurance association was formed. The shipowners' protecting and indemnity associations have lasted all these years and have in the latter stages accepted charterers as members on the basis that they are owners in their own right and are merely chartering in tonnage to augment their existing fleets, so needing an extension of their P & I cover to protect them for their risks as a charterer.

So, if there are established owners' clubs offering cover in respect of protection and indemnity risks to which charterers may under certain circumstances belong, where was the need for a charterers' club and why suddenly in the year 1986 did the idea emerge to start one? The simple answer to that question is that there *was* a need. Charterer members of owners' clubs are a minority group and constitute, generally speaking, and in almost every individual case, a conflict of interests with the majority membership. Thus the idea of a club exclusively for charterers with only charterers as members and with the management of the association geared to their interests only was an attractive notion.

So it was that on 20 February 1986 the club opened for defence cover only (full liability cover followed in the second year of operation on 1 January 1987) and membership was offered to all categories of charterers, whether voyage, time, space or slot but not including demise or bareboat charterers since the latter, by the very nature of the charter-party terms, were more suited to membership of an owners' club.

The charterers' club offers two classes of insurance cover: class I—defence and class 2—liability. Much emphasis is placed on the benefits provided by the defence class of cover which is a departure from the traditional view taken by the managers of the shipowners' long-established P & I clubs that the predominant class of cover is the P & I and the defence class is only an adjunct of that. The latter might have been a perfectly logical view before the serious rise in legal costs which has taken place since World War II, but it is that very rise which has thrown defence cover into greater prominence. More and more owners and charterers are realising the need to be protected against the legal costs of resolving charter-party disputes, particularly in an age when more and more owners and charterers are litigation conscious and are anxious to take their opponents to arbitration or the courts in respect of even a minimal amount of money. Because the cost of legal services is high, even the cost of obtaining an opinion, the role of defence club managers is itself becoming more important since it is to them that club members turn in the first instance to help them out of a legal or even a practical problem. The managers of the charterers' club realised early on that defence cover is a type of cover which cannot be obtained in the ordinary insurance market and even if it could be obtained, the market insurers could not provide the claims handling service and legal advice which club managers are traditionally trained to give through their own qualified staff.

The advantages to charterers of having their own club offering defence cover based in London, the same city as many of the owners' defence clubs, must be plainly seen. The existence of an exclusively charterers' club in London as a negotiating forum in charter-party disputes should be of not inconsiderable value and must be geographically well placed to play its part in minimising the incurring of legal expenses and in keeping a watch over the process of litigation and/or arbitration into which charterers may enter in protection of their rights and entitlements under their charter-party contracts.

The reader may find it useful to have a résumé of the sort of risks/liabilities to which a charterer is exposed in the course of his chartering operations and see how the range of liabilities compares with that of an owner. We shall study charterers who do not possess or control the ship, i.e. who are *not* bareboat or demise charterers but who are chartering on a time or voyage basis. The demise (or bareboat) charterer being in control of the ship by virtue of employment of master and crew, incurs risks as wide as an owner since he runs not only employment risks but navigational risks as well. His P & I insurance is therefore better placed in an owners' club. Regarding other charterers, the risk which springs most obviously to mind, and this would refer particularly to voyage charterers, and the one which is probably highest in value of any of the risks which a charterer faces, is that of damaging the vessel due to a breach of the safe berth or safe port warranties. This could result in a total loss as well as a partial loss. The definition of a safe port is wide and includes not only the aspect of weather conditions or the physical characteristics of the port, but also the possibility of the port being unsafe for a political reason, e.g. a riot or insurrection. It is also quite possible that apart from the ship itself being damaged by reason of an unsafe berth or port, the cargo carried in the ship could suffer damage as a result of the same cause of action and thus a charterer could find himself liable on two counts, ship and cargo. His liability to cargo interests would not necessarily be direct but more likely indirect by way of indemnity as a result of charter-party stipulations in favour of the ship's owners who might have had to pay out directly to the owners of the cargo under the terms and conditions of their bill of lading, identifying them, the owners, as carriers.

The wording of the rule relevant to liability in respect of damage to an entered ship reads as follows: 'to indemnify an owner or a disponent owner under the terms of a charter-party of an entered ship or to pay to an owner or a disponent owner damages or compensation (including detention and/or demurrage and/or hire) which may arise out of physical loss or damage to an entered ship, to include loss or damage to hull, machinery, containers (if owned or leased by such owner or disponent owner), equipment, stores, fuel, supplies or other property of such owner or disponent owner on board such entered ship'. There are two provisos, first, that such property is not within the scope of the rule relating to cargo liabilities or within any proviso, exclusion, limit or deductible applicable to that section and, secondly, that such property is not owned or leased by the member or by any company associated with or under the same management as the member.

It will be seen readily that the above rule would be sufficient to cover a charterer member in respect of a claim based on the provision of sub-standard bunkers to a vessel by a time charterer which resulted in the ship's engines being harmed or damaged as a result of the poor quality. This type of loss and/or claim is becoming more frequent and it is a practice of these modern times that where there is an engine breakdown a shipowner may look and see where he may place the blame and if bunkers have been supplied to his ship by a time charterer under the terms and conditions of the charter-party, he may well try and establish a link between the poor quality bunkers, if such are found to be, and the damage caused to his ship.

This leads naturally on to the subject of bills of lading. Where English law applies, it is generally the practice that bills of lading are 'owners' bills'. In being signed by or on behalf of the master (who is the servant in law of the owners) they form the backbone of a contract of carriage between the owners and the shipper of the goods and/or the eventual indorsee of the bill of lading. This concept is reinforced by the recognition by the English courts as valid and enforceable of the so-called 'demise' or 'identity of carrier' clause purporting to allow a time charterer of a vessel who is using his own bill of lading form with his own logo to opt out of being principal party to the bill of lading contract on the ground of his being an agent only and thus under no personal liability to the bill of lading holder. However, the charterer could well still be liable under the terms and conditions of the charter-party if those terms laid upon him legal liability for the consequences of, e.g. the negligent loading, stowing, discharge or trimming of the goods which is very often the case in commonly used charter-party forms. It would be either a very unwise or a very affluent charterer who in chartering ships to carry cargo owned by third parties, did not take out liability insurance to cover this particular risk. Even in a predominantly charterers' market it would be a very rare charter-party indeed whose clauses gave the charterer absolute and complete protection against any possible liability towards cargo.

Although English jurisdiction is widely favoured under freedom of choice principles, there are plenty of countries where the law decrees that the charterer *is* the carrier of the goods, particularly where the charterer is using his own bill of lading form and the document is signed by himself or his agent albeit by way of the master's authority. The original Hague Rules and the Hague-Visby Rules are both careful to leave the question of 'who is the carrier' unanswered, since the answer does depend entirely on which jurisdiction is involved in the dispute. French and German jurisdictions, for example, tend to regard the charterer as the carrier basing their judicial views rather more upon which party issued the bill; certain parts of the United States take the same view. Therefore, if a time charterer is trading more or less on a worldwide basis, he would have to realise that his exposure to cargo claims resulted from two sources: (a) the direct source, either cargo-owner or underwriter against him directly as carrier or (b) exposure by way of indemnity under the charter-party to the owner who may have had to pay out cargo claim money to the cargo-owner or his underwriter. In whichever of these two ways the charterer is exposed, charterers' liability under the club rules covers both eventualities.

Charterers of ships carrying liquid cargoes are not exposed to the risk of damaging the cargo as are their dry cargo counterparts. By its very nature there is little harm that can be done to oil during the sea transit period other than contamination and that particular type of harm is unlikely to be attributable to the charterer's fault. Straight cargo shortages where quantities short of the bill of lading figures are delivered are also most likely to be an owner's risk.

The third risk, after hull and cargo loss/damage, to which a charterer may be exposed is injury or death to persons on or near the ship. Again oil charterers are unlikely to find themselves liable for causing personal injury either to members of the crew or maritime shore workers working on board because of the absence of any handling process, that is, a manual process. It is only in the context of stevedoring operations for the handling of dry cargo on and off ship that such accidents are likely to occur. As with cargo risks, a charterer may find himself liable ultimately by way of indemnity under the charter-party. One of the most prolific jurisdictions for P & I personal injury claims is that of the USA. This is not because there are necessarily more accidents than elsewhere, though the USA does maintain a massive coastline containing more ports than most other countries, but because US law allows injured maritime workers, whether crew or shore workers, to seek remedies through the courts independently of any statutory compensation which they may be entitled to irrespective of whether there has been fault. The shipowner, whose ship was the scene of the accident, is primarily in the firing line and is likely to be the party sued for damages by the injured man. He would have to prove negligence to succeed in his claim. The charterer might be also sued direct though this is unlikely because it is not his ship and his identity is less likely to be readily available.

However, after the shipowner is condemned to pay damages by a US district court award for example, he may elect to institute an indemnity action against the charterer under the arbitration agreement (be it in London or New York). In recent years there have been several successful attempts by shipowners against charterers under the Baltime and NYPE charter-parties containing a London arbitration agreement.

One example of such a successful recovery by a shipowner was following upon an accident suffered by a US longshoreman in the port of Seattle where prior to discharge the steel pontoons were being swung off the hatches and landed by the winches in a pile on the deck beside the hatch. The injured man was one of a gang of four longshoremen directing the positioning of these pontoons, and pieces of dunnage wood were positioned slantwise so that they supported the bottom pontoon and kept it off the level of the deck, the other end of the dunnage wood being positioned on one of the adjacent bitts so that the dunnage wood itself was not flat on the deck. When about the fourth pontoon landed on the pile one of these pieces of dunnage wood broke under the weight and the pile of four pontoons crashed to the deck crushing the toes of the injured man in the process since he was standing close to the pile and had no time to jump clear. The vessel at the time was chartered under a 'Baltime' charter-party containing a London arbitration clause. The charter-party also contained various clauses which expressly allowed the owners to obtain indemnity from the charterers for the consequences of their master obeying the orders of the charterer in connection with the employment of the ship. The stevedores are employed by the charterer and it was the charterer who was obliged to bear vicarious responsibility for the acts, neglects and defaults of the stevedores during the course of their stevedoring operations. The injured man obtained a court award against the shipowner for US$93,000. This amount would have been more but the trial jury found that the man himself had to bear 25% responsibility for his own accident.

Subsequent to the primary action in the United States the shipowner commenced arbitration in London to seek recovery of the amount of the award plus costs from the time charterer. By variation of the arbitration agreement Lord Denning was selected by both parties as sole arbitrator and in a hearing which lasted one day only he made his award in favour of the owners in that the proximate cause of the man's accident and resulting injury was the order of the charterers that the vessel proceed to Seattle for discharge and that there had been no break in the chain of causation. This was despite an ingenious attempt by the charterers' lawyers to show that there had been a break in that the cause of the owners' loss was not so much the ordering of the vessel to Seattle by the charterers but rather an erroneous judgment of the district court in Seattle and/or an erroneous decision of the jury to find liability on the part of the owners whereas there should have been no liability at all on their part in that the stevedores were employed on board by the charterers, were acting on their own initiative and totally under their own control and there were no ship's officers on the scene or directing the operations at the material time.

This particular case, and two or three similar ones at about the same time have indicated clearly that time charterers of vessels, particularly those which trade to and from the United States are exposed to the risk of liability for death or personal injury either by being sued direct or by being sued by way of indemnity under an arbitration agreement in the charter-party. The remainder of the traditional P & I risks, e.g. collision risks, oil pollution risks, fines, irrecoverable GA, etc., to be found in the P & I rules of an owners' club (and indeed also to be found listed under the ordinary liability cover obtainable from the charterers' club) are unlikely to trouble a charterer. Collision, for example, is the result of navigational faults, an exclusively owners' responsibility, not charterers', unless the charter is on demise terms. Japan alone of the world's nations appears to include within its jurisdiction the judicial concept of a charterer being liable for collision damage.

Although the owners' clubs do accept charterers into membership as 'special entries' on fixed premium terms, the practice of admitting them as members is something of an illogicality and could perhaps be compared to a sports club admitting to its membership players of opposing teams. Owners and charterers are on opposite sides of the contractual fence and even if they may sometimes occupy common ground in fighting third parties, they may nevertheless easily find themselves on opposite sides of the 'claims' field in a charter-party dispute. A further point is that owners' clubs are third-party liability insurers and charterers require more than that. They also require cover for their liability for damaging the vessel through, e.g. breach of the safe port warranty or safe berth clause. This is first or second party liability. The owners' clubs, as has been seen, exclude, specifically, damage to the entered vessel within their ordinary cover and yet, paradoxically, a charterer most definitely needs this type of cover is he is put at risk for damaging the ship he has chartered by reason of the inclusion in his charter-party (which will almost invariably be the case) of a safe port warranty or a safe berth clause. Owners' clubs are not geared within the ordinary rules to provide this additional cover and they would, if asked to do so, have need to purchase it for a charterer from the open market. The charterers' club offers a package which includes hull, cargo and residual P & I risks all within one P & I policy, together with an 'optional extra' of loss of bunkers (for time charterers whose property bunkers will likely be).

One other major difference between the cover provided to or available for time or voyage charterers and that for owners is the limit of cover given. We have seen that the scope, although similar on paper, differs as to the degree of exposure to individual risks. However, the limit is not the unlimited cover given by the group clubs to their owner members. Charterers, whether they seek cover with an owners' club as a 'special entry' or whether they look to the 'comprehensive package' offered by the charterers' association, will find a limit placed on their cover. There is sound logic in this. An owner, because of his ownership of his ship, is exposed to liability for the huge destruction that a ship can wreak upon third parties' lives or property. Consider the devastation that two fully loaded super tankers may cause if they collide in a waterway running near to a highly populated industrial area. The damage will be at best catastrophic, at worst unthinkable, and it is reflected in the 'overspill' arrangements beyond the cut-off point of the excess loss reinsurance contract arranged by the International Group of P & I clubs. Charterers should never be exposed to these massive liabilities.

Exclusions from charterers' cargo liability cover are broadly the same as are to be found in an owners' club rules in the comparable position. The exclusions in connection with bills of lading would be relevant to a charterers' cover in those jurisdictions where the charterer is considered to be the bill of lading carrier despite the presence of an identity of carrier clause in the bill of lading purporting to deny this and regardless of whether the document is signed by or for the master on his authority.

WAR RISKS CLUBS

In the early years of the protection and indemnity associations there was cover for shipowners in respect of risks and liabilities which were not insurable elsewhere. It was market practice that all policies of marine insurance on hull and machinery contained a clause which excluded war risks from the cover provided. As a result of this there was considerable sympathy for owners in consequence of this situation as it was in hull and machinery insurance policies that there was an FC & S clause (free of capture and seizure) which was an exclusion incorporated into the policies so that insurers could rate the insurance on the particular vessel without taking into account war risks. At that time, if war risks cover was required, it had to be specifically requested by the assured and the appropriate war rate was then charged. Accordingly, hull and machinery policies enabled underwriters to exclude cover for losses by capture or seizure by enemy ships.

Further, it was clearly apparent that the ordinary rules of all P & I associations were framed in such a way that they only covered liability through the ownership of the vessel, that is, damage done to other ships or property and cargo carried but not any risks or liabilities of the hull and machinery of the vessel itself.

P & I associations would not indemnify an owner against any liabilities, or any costs or expenses arising, when there was any loss or damage, injury, illness or death or other accident which was caused by any of the following:

1. War, civil war, revolution, rebellion, insurrection or civil strife arising therefrom, or any hostile act by or against a belligerent power.
2. Capture, seizure, arrest, restraint or detainment and the consequences thereof or any attempts thereat.
3. Mines, torpedoes, bombs, rockets, shells, explosive or any other similar weapons of war.

Accordingly, the only way that shipowners could seek assistance from the P & I associations was for the shipowners to form special war risk classes in the association which the protection and indemnity members could join if they so wished. However, in the early 1900s, these first war risk classes received little support and those who did join hesitated at having to pay calls for a policy which had to be stamped with a costly *ad valorem* stamp duty and for which there was no visible risk. Indeed, at that time there were no reinsurance facilities for any portion of the war risk cover that was available.

This position remained in limbo until about 1912, when in the United Kingdom the Chancellor of the Exchequer introduced into the Finance Act a notice abolishing heavy *ad valorem* duty on insurance policies. The effect of this was to enable the mutual clubs to restore the facility of war risks insurance for shipowners and this had the effect of relieving shipowners' worst fears of being uninsured should there be an outbreak of war, during which ships at sea could be exposed to extreme war perils.

Obviously these risks were too great for just one club to bear on its own as they could involve the members in very high premiums without reinsurance if war did come. It was decided, therefore, that the P & I clubs would pool their resources and seven P & I clubs did just this and commenced operation on 20 February 1912 reinsuring each other for the full values insured in the war risks associations.

The cover provided by the early P & I associations was for risks excluded from the marine insurance policies by the FC & S clause. The cost of such insurance was extremely cheap and shipowners realised that there was merit in having such cheap insurance which was, although limited in scope, good value. Some of the P & I clubs operated the insurance from a new separate class whilst others formed separate war risk clubs themselves, as a separate entity.

When a war involving Britain was contemplated the UK Government was concerned at the impossible position of British shipowners being unable to obtain full war risks insurance in a time of war to enable them to carry on their normal business activities. The Government appointed a sub-committee of the Committee of Imperial Defence to inquire into this situation. It issued its report in April 1914. Insurance against war risks at that time could only be obtained from the war risks associations for ships that were at sea at the outbreak of war and until they arrived in a safe port. However, it was realised that in order to enable the life of the country to continue and to supply armed forces at home and overseas it was essential for the Government to assist the war risk associations to extend their insurances by affording them reinsurance to a reasonable extent.

A suitable scheme was drawn up and in July 1914 when a world war appeared imminent the war risk associations were asked to co-operate in carrying out the scheme in consideration of the Government reinsuring the war risk associations to the extent of 80% of every British vessel they insured, the premiums being fixed by agreement between the Government and the clubs for periods of 91 days on a single or round voyage basis.

Following the outbreak of war in August 1914 the scheme as outlined came into operation and the agreement with the war risk clubs was signed. At that time, insured values for war risks had to be increased from time to time to take account of rising costs of construction and the high values of neutral flag ships, which could earn huge profits in what was then an uncontrolled freight market.

The scheme worked very well and was able to ensure that shipowners, having suffered serious losses during the war, continued in the industry and the war risk associations may experience a great deal of satisfaction in that they afforded such valuable assistance to British shipping during two world wars when shipping itself was one of the prime objects of attack.

War risk associations whether forming a class within a P & I club or mutual war risk associations, have existed ever since and have developed and prospered. Mutual war risk associations operate on a non-profit making basis, which means that the risks which are insured with the club are shared equitably amongst the members of the club. By this means each member is, in fact, insuring and is insured by the other members.

As with other forms of war risks insurance the basic cover is for risks excluded from the hull and machinery and/or freight and disbursements policies by clauses 23, 24 and 25 of the Institute Time Clauses (Hulls), namely 'the war exclusion', 'strikes exclusion' and the 'malicious acts exclusion' including capture, seizure, arrest, restraint or detainment, civil war, civil strife, mines, torpedoes, bombs, etc., strikers and other persons engaged in labour commotions or the detonation of an explosive by persons acting maliciously. In addition, members will benefit from extremely wide cover for detention and detainment:

(a) To avoid loss or damage to the ship arising from a war risk.
(b) To comply with orders, directions or recommendations by the directors or by any government department of the country in which the ship is owned, managed or registered or of any country having the right to give such orders, prohibitions, directions or recommendations or by the military authority of such country given in order to avoid loss of or damage to the entered ship by a war risk.
(c) By persons engaged in war, civil war or rebellion.

(d) By persons acting from a political motive.

Another aspect of the cover of particular note is cover against detention or trapping. In these circumstances, if the insured vessel is detained by any of the above-mentioned risks for less than 90 days, the member recovers running expenses for a period of detention, but if that period exceeds 90 days then, generally speaking, the member may also additionally recover from his war risk association a sum calculated at the rate of 10% per annum of the value of the entered ship pro rata over the period of detention, unless or until the ship becomes an actual or constructive total loss. This type of cover obviously proved extremely useful to vessels which became trapped in the Shatt Al Arab river as a result of the hostilities of the Iran–Iraq war in 1980. It is also worthy of note that if an actual or constructive total loss arises by capture, seizure, arrest, restraint or detainment, the association will be able to pay a total loss within months of the date of the incident.

Another area in which the member of the war risk association can enjoy extremely wide cover is in relation to the P & I claims arising out of or in consequence of a war risk—for example, claims that would be excluded by the normal P & I cover by the war exclusion clause. The risks covered under such a section would include the usual categories of loss of life, personal injury, illness, expenses consequent upon shipwreck, expenses in respect of captured or detained crew, collision, damage to fixed and floating objects, wreck removal and cargo claims.

There have been in recent times, particularly as a result of the Iran–Iraq hostilities, large increases in claims activity. However, the mutual war risk club concept has been able to hold additional premiums for better trading in such a war zone at very competitive levels when compared with other insurance markets. This has been due in the main to a successful investment programme for the club's reserves and first class collaboration with reinsurers and brokers, but above all continuing loyalty and support by the members themselves.

It is of extreme importance that good collaboration with insurers and the sound placing of reinsurance are maintained to continue the well-being of the war risk associations. Obviously, if a war risk club was faced with a run of heavy claims it could raise additional money needed to pay such claims by increasing the amount of supplementary contributions. Such a policy, however, would mean some appreciable fluctuation in the amount of supplementary contributions that it may charge from year to year. For example, in a very good year supplementary contributions would not be needed at all, indeed, a return of call might be appropriate. In a bad year, however, large supplementary contributions may be required and this would be unacceptable to the majority of members. Like most other commercial undertakings insurance costs are closely monitored and budgeted, and it would therefore be somewhat inconvenient if sometime after the expiry of the trading year to which the particular budget refers the members were to receive from the club an invoice for supplementary contributions considerably in excess of the amount originally estimated. To counteract such a situation developing the war risk associations would arrange reinsurance, the primary purpose of which is to protect the membership from dramatic fluctuations in the level of supplementary contributions from one year to the next. Normally, a war risk mutual would purchase reinsurance on an excess-of-loss basis, which means that all payments in excess of a given figure would be borne by the reinsurer. The point at which the amount of risk to be retained is fixed by the association can always be a matter of judgment depending in part on the club's premium income, its claims experience and the amount of premium charged by the reinsuring underwriters.

We have mentioned earlier with regard to the protection and indemnity associations that they will not indemnify an owner against any liabilities, costs or expenses, when the loss or damage, injury, illness or death or any other accident in respect of which such a liability will arise was caused by a variety of war and warlike situations. However, the International Group of P & I Associations decided that with effect from 20 February 1987 policy year they would provide to their members a 'special cover' for war risks insurance. Such special cover is supported by separate reinsurance from underwriters. The P & I associations advise that in some difficult cases a member may not be certain whether or not the normal P & I war risks exclusion would apply to the particular circumstances of an incident. Should this uncertainty continue even after an incident has occurred, the P & I club member may be left in doubt as to whether his claim is covered by the association or not. Similarly, there are borderline situations between circumstances in which a claim can be paid by the association and those in which a similar claim is excluded, for example, when there is terrorist activity. Recent experiences have suggested that incidents falling within the definition of 'war risks' are becoming more and more frequent and they are by no means confined to areas where it is known that an armed conflict is in progress.

There are many members of the P & I clubs that will have some cover against P & I liabilities from their war risk underwriters. However, it is quite possible that the wording of the relevant war risk policy may not exactly mirror the wording of the P & I club's exclusion. Furthermore, the coverage available from war risk underwriters is normally subject to a limit of liability, sometimes set at a relatively low level. Therefore, this additional cover for war risk situations, being given by the P & I clubs, will cover such claims that are excluded under the normal P & I association war risk exclusion rule. This additional coverage from the clubs would respond only to the extent of what each and every member is unable to recover from his normal war risk policies. The amount recoverable from the war risk underwriter would operate as a deductible applying to the special cover given by the P & I clubs. Indeed, this special cover would in itself be limited to a figure of US$50 million for any one accident, each vessel, in excess of the same deductible.

It is clear, therefore, that this additional P & I war risk cover should not replace the existing war risk cover for P & I claims, indeed the clubs are urging their members to maintain their existing war risk P & I cover to the maximum extent available from their war risk underwriters. The special cover from the clubs would therefore operate as an excess cover to the extent that each member is found to be unable to make a full recovery from war risk underwriters.

This special cover provided is in any event subject to the terms equivalent to the institute notice of cancellation and war automatic termination cover clause. This clause provides that cover terminates automatically upon the detonation of a nuclear device, upon the outbreak of war between any of the major powers or upon requisition of the vessel. It also provides for cancellation of cover upon seven days' notice. Although the said institute clause contains a mechanism for reinstating cover upon payment of an additional premium, the P & I associations do not consider it appropriate to become involved in the assessment and collection of additional premiums and it is their intention to protect themselves and their members by the general prohibition of any defined geographical area which, in their opinion, they consider to present an unacceptably high risk. Ships that are within such a prohibited area would not be covered under the association's special cover and their owners would have to rely on whatever other war risk insurance was available to them.

THROUGH TRANSPORT CLUBS

Over the last two decades or so we have seen a revolution in the methods of transportation of cargo by sea through the introduction of consolidated methods of cargo carriage. Such methods have led to the introduction of such concepts as containerisation, palletisation and the roll-on roll-off methods of carriage of goods by sea. The 'through transport' concept was really born in the late 1980s when there was a need to enhance the services offered by regular shipping lines.

From a traditional viewpoint, the liner operator, like his counterpart in the tramp trades, has accepted responsibility for cargo carried during the sea leg of the voyage. Of course, this was all that was required of him under the terms of international conventions and, indeed, to have accepted greater responsibilities would have exposed such an operator to claims which were not covered by shipowners' liability insurers, the P & I clubs themselves.

For a shipper and a receiver of cargo, the attractions of a contract which covered the entire voyage were obvious. Claims for loss of or damage to cargo would be directed against just one contracting carrier and not one of several; therefore, the responsibility for safe delivery of that cargo would be in the hands of one company only and not many. The 'through bill of lading' offered such a contract and P & I clubs, conscious of the need to expand their rules to meet the requirements of the developing shipping industry, extended their rules to provide the cover that was necessary to protect their members' new responsibilities. Perhaps the most obvious risk, and one which the P & I associations cover, is their members' liability arising under the bill of lading for loss of or damage to cargo during the inland transportation part of the voyage. Strictly this is not a mutual risk because the majority of members do not accept responsibility for cargo prior to loading or after discharge. Therefore, the P & I associations, largely as a result of containerisation, met the requirement of insurance for the through transport operator who would undertake the responsibility for the goods regardless of the number of forms of transport employed.

The through transport operator in undertaking his task will be immediately exposed to a number of hazards against which he must obtain relevant insurance to insure him against numerous risks to which he is exposed including the following:

1. Liability to the owner of goods or to the insurer of those goods if the owner has subrogated his rights.
2. Liability to third parties.
3. Loss of or damage to the equipment that the through transport operator owns or leases.

The main types of through transport operator who require such insurance comprise the following:

1. Shipowners and charterers.
2. Port terminal and inland depot operators.
3. Freight forwarders and non-vessel operating carriers.
4. Container lessors.

Whether it is the shipowner, charterer or a combined transport operator who is running a unitised service the operator will need to insure the containers, trailers and handling equipment used by him. If the insured is the owner of such equipment he will, of course, want to protect his investment and similarly, where the equipment is leased on hire, the leasing company as a condition of the lease, may require that the equipment be insured. Additionally, the operator of such equipment will incur third-party liabilities and other ancillary risks arising out of the operation of the equipment and the mutual clubs will provide insurance of these risks and provide a package to suit the operator's business and needs.

A summary of the cover is as follows:

Handling equipment: cover for 'all risks' of loss or damage; this can be limited to total loss only, if desired, and can also include war risks and strikes, riots and civil commotions risks, subject to agreed wording.

Contributions in general average or salvage.

Third-party liabilities: loss of or damage to third-party property other than cargo, death, injury or illness of any person other than an employee.

Liabilities to authorities: wreck removal of equipment following an accident.

Quarantine and disinfection of equipment.

Fines, other financial penalties and customs duty in respect of a breach of regulations relating to:

(a) The import or export of equipment to or from a country.

(b) Safety of working conditions.

Insurance of costs and expenses: legal and other costs incurred in investigating or minimising liability.

Insurance for container terminals and depots: marine terminals, inland clearance depots, container freight stations, container storage depots will all incur contractual liabilities to their customers. Further legal liabilities to third parties will be incurred and have at risk the handling equipment with which they perform their operations.

With regard to contractual liabilities, marine container terminal operators provide services against the background of increasing legal and commercial pressures to accept higher levels of liability for fault or negligence, which indeed result in the need for advice on the levels of such liabilities and, of course, adequate insurance and efficient claims handling.

Insurance for cranes, other handling equipment and trailers: cover ranges from 'all risks' of physical loss or damage to 'total loss only'.

Cover can, if required, include the risks of 'strikes, riots and civil commotions'.

'Machinery breakdown' and 'loss of profits' consequent thereon, subject to agreed wording.

Liabilities in relation to cargo (including customers' containers and trailers): physical loss of or damage to cargo.

Misdirection or misdelivery of cargo.

Delay.

Delivery of cargo contrary to instructions or without production of the bill of lading.

NB the operator is insured under the above even if a court (in any country) sets aside his conditions of business and finds him liable.

Third-party liabilities: loss of or damage to third-party property, other than cargo (including damage to ship). Death, injury or illness of any person other than an employee. Liabilities to authorities: removal of cargo or handling equipment following an accident.

Quarantine and disinfection of cargo and handling equipment.

Fines, other financial penalties, customs duty and confiscation of property.

Insurance for freight forwarders and non-vessel operating carriers: in circumstances where an operator acts as a freight forwarder or indeed as a non-vessel operating carrier the contract between him and his customer is usually subject to his own standard trading conditions of business and, maybe, a house bill of lading.

A freight forwarder will have certain other liabilities in the area of professional negligence. Indeed, there has been a trend in recent years for freight forwarders to accept more responsibility under their trading conditions making them liable for sums which are out of proportion to the profit they may make when undertaking shipments for their customer. It may be, for example, that they are held to be a principal and may find themselves liable without recourse to others.

Through transport mutual insurance associations may specialise in liability insurance for freight forwarders and provide necessary insurance to suit companies trading as freight forwarders. The insurance is designed to cover all operations of a freight forwarder and may be summarised as follows:

Liabilities in relation to cargo

Physical loss of or damage to cargo
Misdirection or misdelivery of cargo
Consequential loss resulting from the above
Delay
Delivery of cargo contrary to instructions or without production of the bill of lading

Other financial loss suffered by the customer as a result of breach of contract.

NB the operator is insured under the above even if a court (in any country) sets aside his trading conditions and finds him fully liable.

Customs liabilities

Fines, other financial penalties or duty (e.g. arising out of customs bonds or 'T' form guarantees).

Third-party liabilities

Loss of or damage to third-party property, other than cargo.
Death, injury or illness of any person other than an employee.
Insurance of containers, trailers and handling equipment: physical loss of or damage to equipment used by the operator whether it belongs to him, a leasing company or a subcontractor.

Contingency insurance for container lessors

Through transport mutual insurance associations can provide insurance cover for container lessors which would cover the main types of insurance such as:

1. Contingency cover for leased containers following the lessee's default (e.g. bankruptcy) in respect of:
   (a) the costs of repossessing containers abandoned by the lessee;
   (b) the costs of repairing damage to the repossessed containers;
   (c) the value of any unrecovered containers.

(Such cover would generally be restricted to lessees designated as 'classified' by the clubs.)

2. All risks of physical loss of and/or damage to containers while they are off lease.
3. Third-party liabilities whether the containers are on lease or off lease.

FURTHER DEVELOPMENTS IN MUTUAL INSURANCE

The shipping industry has seen a substantial decline in its fortunes over recent years having lived through a very deep depression indeed. Fortunately, we are now beginning to see the signs of recovery. However, as a result of this, the mutual clubs, which traditionally have insured members' risks in areas such as protection and indemnity, including a whole range of shipowners' third-party liabilities, strikes insurance and insurance of legal expenses, have seen the market contract considerably with less business available and a substantial reduction in ships to insure.

Obviously during the good years of the 1970s and early 1980s there was plenty of business available for mutual clubs to be well supported. The changes in fortune of world shipping, however, have altered this situation and it is now apparent that the traditional P & I clubs, which provide mutual cover against a variety of risks to an entered member, are attempting to diversify by setting up new mutual organisations wherever there is a new demand for them.

Quite a number of management companies of P & I clubs, because of their experience in mutual liability insurance have been approached by organisations concerning the formation of new mutuals. It is true to say that over recent years we have seen a considerable increase in the claims conscious area of professional indemnity insurance and it is mainly as a result of this that new mutuals have been springing up to fill certain gaps in the insurance market. Traditional club managers have now expanded into new areas where they receive support for the mutual concept in areas of professional indemnity insurance. This type of insurance was previously covered on the general insurance market and, because of rising costs and indeed a considerable increase in claims, this has resulted in the mutuals being better able to compete through their very structure in those traditional markets.

Although there have been mutual clubs in existence to cover the professional liabilities of shipbrokers and agents we have seen their increasing interest in acquiring further mutual cover in the expectation that it will reduce their insurance costs, with the additional advantage of enhancing investment earnings, and obtaining much wider cover and indeed more appropriate cover to meet their individual needs.

More recent developments in new mutuals saw the inauguration of a new mutual for airlines which commenced business from 1 January 1987 with the aim that cover was to be provided to obtain additional capacity for IATA members. The club was incorporated to increase the airlines' influence on aviation insurance rates, policy terms and claims settlements.

Following these developments in the area of professional indemnity insurance new mutual clubs have been started for solicitors, architects, housing associations and the latest being a mutual for barristers.

The new mutual for solicitors was arranged to meet their own particular needs and those of their law practices. This mutual has become a co-insurer with the professional indemnity market which clearly demonstrates the willingness of mutual organisations to diversify from the previously restricted mode of operation in shipping generally.

There have been other such mutuals formed recently and one of the most notable developments in this trend was the 'launching' of a new satellite mutual to cover certain risks related to the European rocket 'Ariane'—a unique and most unusual development.

A new mutual insurance company has been established to provide cover for United Kingdom accountants with the intention of the mutual providing professional indemnity cover for small to medium-sized firms of accountants with the coverage available basically similar in scope to commercial P & I insurance but wider in cover and expenses.

It is obvious that companies in some professions can no longer buy adequate cover for professional indemnity needs in the conventional insurance market. Rates have increased dramatically and cover for their professional indemnity requirements has been consequently reduced. All these aspects have led to the emergence of these captives and mutual insurance organisations.

Undoubtedly the clubs are looking forward to their future expansion and it would appear logical that other professions with possible professional indemnity exposure will come under the microscope. We could speculate that banks, building societies, dentists, doctors, estate agents, financial advisers and many more could be worthy of investigation for potential new mutuals.

It is expected that this trend will continue with expansion into new areas where it is needed, although the traditional P & I associations will undoubtedly continue their important role in providing third-party liability coverage for their traditional shipowning members.

INDEX